THE SUCCESSFUL CO-PARENTING WORKBOOK

THE SUCCESSFUL CO-PARENTING WORKBOOK

Practical Exercises to Heal Yourself and Help Your Kids Thrive

SHERRY L. SMITH, LMFT, CDC®

ROCKRIDGE
PRESS

For general information on our other products and services or to obtain technical support, please contact our Customer Care Department within the United States at (866) 744-2665, or outside the United States at (510) 253-0500.

Rockridge Press publishes its books in a variety of electronic and print formats. Some content that appears in print may not be available in electronic books, and vice versa.

Interior and Cover Designer: Lisa Forde
Art Producer: Melissa Malinowksy
Editor: Andrea Leptinsky
Production Manager: Jose Olivera

All illustrations used under license from Shutterstock and iStock

Paperback ISBN: 978-1-63807-198-3 | eBook ISBN: 978-1-63807-623-0
R0

To my parents, Joe and Peggy Smith,
who were good people dealing with a
high-stress situation in the best way
they knew how. It's because of their
divorce experience that I do this work.

Contents

Introduction

I f you are reading this book, you and your former partner are likely experiencing the end of a relationship and want to protect your child with a set plan on how to continue to parent, together. Welcome to the process that is called "co-parenting." Congratulations to you both for taking the first big step toward ensuring your child will not only survive but thrive through this transition.

When a relationship ends, it is incredibly painful for all members of the family, but especially for your child, who might feel they have no control over their circumstances. Here is an important fact: The trauma in this ending, for your child, is in how the breakup is handled—not the breakup itself. This book will provide you with the tools you need to help you through this transition whether you have one child or multiple children.

I am a Licensed Marriage and Family Therapist and Certified Divorce Coach®. I work with people every day in my private practice who are dealing with the stages of relationships ending. I combine my education and experience in family systems, my training in divorce, and my life experience to help people handle breakups in a way that minimizes trauma to the kids. I'm asked on a regular basis why I choose to do this work. For me, it's a calling. I was a child of a high-conflict divorce, and it took me decades to undo the damage. My parents, may they rest in peace, did everything wrong in their divorce. I mean *everything*! In their defense, there weren't the resources available when they divorced in the early 1980s that are available now.

I found out my parents were splitting up in August of 1982 when I was 17 years old, the day before my senior year of high school. I originally lived with my father, who was in a constant state of rage that he projected onto me. I eventually moved in with my mother, who was living with my aunt Ruth at the time. As much as I loved my aunt and was grateful for the peaceful, stable environment, I felt like a guest in her home. My entire senior year of high school, no one outside of my family knew what was happening. I presented to my classmates, teachers, and friends as if everything was perfectly normal at home. Inside, I was experiencing incredible pain that I self-medicated with alcohol. My parents were so wrapped up in their anger toward each other that neither seemed to notice how much I was suffering. I should have been in therapy, but back then people didn't put their kids in therapy. It was much later and after my own divorce that I decided to dedicate my life to helping people avoid making the same mistakes my parents made.

In my work with my clients, I have come to realize that not all relationships are meant to last forever. Divorces and breakups are going to happen. If your relationship was toxic, by ending the relationship, you are modeling for your child agency and self-respect by moving on and creating a new, healthier life, no matter who made the decision to end the relationship. The old relationship as it was dissolved, and a new relationship has formed.

You both are likely dealing with your own wide range of emotions from the breakup and not feeling grounded or like your best selves when parenting your children. Your children are experiencing the sadness, disappointment, fear, and pain that comes with the end of your relationship, and you are likely experiencing these same emotions. My goal is to offer you a practical step-by-step guide with actionable tools to help you and your co-parent heal yourselves so you can co-parent your child successfully. It all starts with giving your child a secure, safe place where they can express their emotions. The best way to accomplish this is for each of you to honor your own unique healing process and get comfortable with your own emotions and vulnerability so you can sit with your child as they express theirs.

In this book, you will learn about best practices in co-parenting, as well as exercises and interventions that both co-parents can use together to help you heal and provide a joined, united co-parenting relationship for your child. This can be a difficult process, so you'll find Positivity Pauses to help you maintain a positive mindset as you work through the book. This book is broken down into steps, with each chapter acting as a building block to help you develop your new co-parenting plan. This plan will be the foundation of your co-parenting relationship. You'll learn about what co-parenting is and what goes into a good co-parenting plan. As you work through the exercises, you'll be given tools to better anticipate and manage conflict and improve communication. You'll also learn how you both can help your child thrive through the process by turning this painful experience into an opportunity to build their emotional intelligence. By the time you finish the workbook, not only will you have the assurance that comes with creating a solid co-parenting plan, but you will also have the tools to heal yourselves and help your child heal, too. There might be readers of this book who are dealing with a toxic ex. Although this book is designed to be used by both co-parents, it also has tools for people who feel that co-parenting with their ex isn't possible.

Doing the work outlined in this book won't be easy. After all, personal growth is never easy, but there's always a payoff at the end. You both wouldn't be willing to do the work if you didn't love your kids and want what's best for them. You are to be commended for having the courage to embark on this journey together. You will realize that your hard work has paid off when you both have the peace of mind that comes with having planned for every aspect of your child's well-being. Let's embark together on your journey to heal yourselves and, in turn, create a healthy co-parenting relationship for your children!

PART ONE

Successful Co-Parenting

CHAPTER ONE

Co-Parenting 101

In this chapter, you will learn how to navigate the early stages of your co-parenting relationship, and you will acquire actionable strategies to make your co-parenting relationship successful. When you and your partner ended the relationship, the family did not end—it just took on a different form. Children thrive when they have good routine and structure in a loving, nurturing environment. This can be created in two households if you are joined and united co-parents. As you grow and evolve in your relationship as co-parents, your child will benefit both from having the security of parents with a solid co-parenting relationship and from watching you model healthy communication skills. The tools that this chapter provides will not only help improve your co-parenting relationship, but will also have an impact on all your relationships.

Creating a New Parenting Relationship

Now that your romantic relationship is ending, it might be difficult to envision what a new platonic one would look like. In typical breakup scenarios, partners have time to grieve, reflect, and implement personal life changes before moving on. When a child is involved, however, that path forward takes a different route. Instead, one of your first steps as two separated adults is to form a co-parenting relationship. Make no mistake, this relationship is centered around the betterment, support, and security of your child or children. For it to work, personal issues and past experiences from your time as a couple should be left at the door.

The new co-parenting relationship will be different from the previous partnered relationship: The dynamic will change significantly, as will the way you view each other. This means that you will both need to be willing to compartmentalize your feelings about the issues that occurred between the two of you and be open to forming a new relationship that is strictly focused on your child's well-being. The good news is that by being open to the concept of co-parenting, you both are also opening up to the idea that you aren't alone in parenting your child.

Making this shift is easy for some people and challenging for others. It's normal to experience some negative feelings around what happened before the breakup, such as hurt, betrayal, abandonment, or even guilt. If you feel you are harboring emotions from the past that present an obstacle to embarking on a new co-parenting relationship, you will find resources to help you work through that in this book. Your new co-parenting relationship will establish boundaries for communication, whether you decide to communicate via phone or use a form of written communication daily or less frequently. You'll learn what situations warrant what type of communication. You will also both agree on pick-up and drop-off arrangements and how to interact with each other when you are with your child. Having these boundaries will help you view this relationship in a new and healthy way.

Using this book and working together will help you develop a new co-parenting relationship. This typically isn't an overnight change, but as long as you are both open to the possibility, with patience and perseverance, it can happen. Not only will your child thrive in the process, but you both will also benefit from the personal growth that comes from investing in your own healing.

Role Models and Co-Parenting

Think about a positive role model from your own childhood, such as a parent, family member, or trusted adult. Who was that person? Describe the impact they had on your life.

_____

_____

_____

What strengths do you feel co-parents pull from in order to put their child first?

_____

_____

_____

Describe your ideal co-parenting relationship. Include how you would feel if you were living this ideal.

_____

_____

_____

_____

_____

_____

_____

_____

Making Co-Parenting Successful

In this section, you will learn strategies for managing your emotions so that when you need to show up for your child, you will feel more grounded, present, and emotionally regulated. In addition, as you embark on the journey of creating a co-parenting relationship with new dimensions, it's important to deal with the feelings that go along with your romantic relationship ending so you can put what happened behind you. This starts with being honest about what you are feeling. Often, individuals will deny or distract themselves from their negative emotions. This leads to feeling ungrounded and unfocused, which is counterproductive to putting your child first.

You will also explore the best practices recommended to provide a joined, united, team-based approach to co-parenting, which will create an environment conducive to healthy brain development for your child while also allowing them to focus on being a kid. Your new co-parenting relationship will be one where you speak respectfully about each other in front of your child while being flexible enough to embrace different parenting styles and respect the bond each of you shares with your child.

Putting Your Child First

In the early stages of a romantic relationship ending, the pain can be overwhelming. Your thoughts may be consumed with the breakup and how it happened, who did what to whom, and the timeline of the relationship itself and events that played out throughout the relationship. Getting out of bed and functioning throughout the day may be challenging. During this time, your thoughts may not be on how to create a co-parenting relationship with the other person. If you chose the breakup, perhaps you are feeling some relief mixed in with some fear and anxiety about the future and what it will look like to start all over again. Children are very intuitive and sense more than most adults think they do. Your child may pick up on the fact that you are distracted when you are caring for them, even if you think you have hidden it from them.

During this time, it is crucial to put your children and their well-being at the forefront of every decision, even as uncertainty lingers. The decisions you both make starting now will not only lay the groundwork for your new joined and united co-parenting relationship, but will also have a long-lasting impact on your child's life. In order to be intentional with how you express your feelings, you will need to create time and space for yourself to feel all the feelings during a time when you aren't responsible for taking care of your child. You will learn more about handling your grief in chapter 6. If you each are intentional about how you express your feelings, you will be better able to access the more logical part of your brain and make good, grounded decisions with your child at the forefront of your mind. It will also help you both stay present when you are caring for your child.

A Team-Based Approach

Children learn emotional regulation, including skills to identify and communicate feelings and needs, when they are in a loving, nurturing environment with good routine and structure. According to Salvador Minuchin, the researcher behind Structural Family Therapy, which is one of the foremost models of family therapy used today, "Only the family, society's smallest unit, can change and yet maintain enough continuity to rear children who will not be 'strangers in a strange land,' who will be rooted firmly enough to grow and adapt." It is possible to create this environment while co-parenting using a team-based approach. As parents raising children from two homes, it is important to get on the same page with rules, boundaries, and discipline. If you aren't joined and united in your co-parenting, children will sense this, and it will cause them stress. Either they will become parentified, taking on responsibility for adult feelings and emotions before they are developmentally ready, or they will try to manipulate the situation to their advantage. From the child's perspective, disjointed parenting may seem like an opportunity to manipulate one or both parents, but this behavior is actually just a demonstration of the child's stress.

To create the structure for a team-based approach, be open to sitting down together and writing out a parenting plan that includes rules and boundaries, as well as specific ways you will discipline the children when they break the rules. It's best to create the plan when you aren't upset with something your child did and are both in a calm and logical place. We'll cover specifics around how to create your plan and what to include later in this book.

Once you have a parenting plan in place, you can be somewhat consistent across households. For example, let's say Mom caught Susie sneaking out of the house past her curfew. As punishment, Mom took Susie's iPad away right before she was about to go to her dad's house. Mom can call Dad and explain why she took Susie's iPad away, and Dad can follow through on this discipline at his house.

Leaving the Past Behind

When any relationship ends, there is a period of adjustment. It's important for you to give each other grace as you move through this period. Investing time and energy now into moving toward a "new normal" will help everyone get through the transition. This will require a willingness to put the issues that occurred in the relationship behind you and be open to forming a new relationship. Reframing the relationship in your mind as a totally new dynamic can help you with the process of putting the past behind you.

It takes about three years for the family system to reach a new normal after a breakup. There are exceptions, but generally this is the timeline of healing for most families dealing with separation or divorce: The theme of the first year is "What the heck just happened?" The theme of year two is "Let's fix what we did wrong in year one." Generally, by year three the family system is settling into the new normal. The bulk of the change happens in those first two years. It's around the end of the second year that people recovering from separation will start to get the bounce back in their step and appear ready to think about and plan for the future.

To be clear, the implication here is not to suggest that you wait three years to establish a joined and united co-parenting relationship. Early intervention is crucial when it comes to co-parenting, and this book is designed to help you navigate the new relationship. It's helpful to understand where you both are emotionally so you can compartmentalize your feelings and keep yourself logical, fact-based, future-oriented, and in the here and now rather than focused on what happened prior to the breakup. If you give yourselves space to process your feelings, you will be more able to stay in the logical part of your brain while conversing and will be less likely to bait each other into an argument about the past, which is not productive.

Embracing Different Parenting Styles

As you are thinking about how to form a united co-parenting relationship, you are likely considering how your different parenting styles might be an obstacle. Please be assured that you don't have to create the exact same environment in each home. There can be variations in how you both parent. In fact, these differences can be beneficial for the child, if you are willing to embrace the differences and not criticize the other parent in front of the child. As long as each parent is focused on the child's well-being and the parenting styles are not too far apart, this new family dynamic can instill in the child different values that will benefit them later in life and allow them to have a unique relationship with each parent.

You can establish a unified front by taking a collaborative approach where you both imagine an ideal co-parenting relationship. It's also helpful to imagine what values you want to teach your child, where you are aligned in those values, and where you are different but might complement each other. Once you are clear on each other's ideal co-parenting relationship and the kind of children you want to raise and put out into the world, establish goals on how to get there that embrace your differences. If acrimony exists in the relationship, you can get there by putting your child at the forefront of your intentions. Consider how your feelings about the events that occurred in your relationship prior to the breakup may be affecting your view of each other as a parent. If so, set aside those feelings and focus purely on the other person's relationship with the child and how the child benefits from it. It's helpful to imagine that you are literally sitting in your child's shoes and seeing the relationship from their perspective. Embracing the differences also allows each person to parent the way they want to without fear of being criticized or creating conflict.

Respecting Parental Bonds

Sometimes, when you're trying to co-parent and the other parent makes choices you don't agree with, it can be tempting to bad-mouth that parent in front of the child. Criticizing the other parent in front of your child only creates a loyalty bind and makes them feel conflicted about where to put their love. This can be extremely stressful. In addition, on a subconscious level, your child may be aware of similar qualities they have inherited from the other parent and may feel as though they are being criticized as well. It's crucial that both parents stay on the same page about fostering their child's secure attachment to each parent. That starts by understanding why attachment is so important in child development.

Attachment Theory, originated by John Bowlby and later expanded on by Mary Ainsworth, is a theory grounded in decades of research. It states that the way in which children relate to their primary caregiver creates an attachment style that they carry throughout their lives. One's personal attachment style plays a significant role in who they pick as their partner and how they show up in all their relationships.

According to Robert Karen, PhD, in his book *Becoming Attached*, there are three main attachment styles: ambivalent/anxious, avoidant, and secure.

Ambivalent/Anxious: *"I find others are reluctant to get as close as I would like. I often worry that my partner doesn't really love me or won't want to stay with me. I want to merge completely with another person, and this desire sometimes scares other people away."*

Avoidant: *"I am somewhat uncomfortable being close to others; I find it difficult to trust them completely and to allow myself to depend on others. I am nervous when anyone gets too close, and often, love partners want me to be more intimate than I am comfortable with."*

Secure: *"I find it relatively easy to get close to others and am comfortable depending on them and having them depend on me. I often don't worry about being abandoned or about someone getting too close to me."*

A secure attachment is created when the child feels consistently nurtured and loved by each parent and there is good routine and structure in the home.

Ambivalent, anxious, and avoidant attachments are considered insecure styles and are created when primary caregivers aren't consistently emotionally or physically available, caregivers are overly anxious or enmeshed, there is domestic violence in the home, or the child seeks comfort from but is also afraid of their parent. In general, these styles arise when love given from their primary caretaker is inconsistent or nonexistent.

Recognizing that your child benefits from having a healthy attachment to both parents will help you resist the urge to speak poorly about each other in front of your child, and it will also inspire you to take a more collaborative approach with your co-parent. Your child benefits the most when you speak in positive terms about each other in front of them and encourage your child to share their positive feelings about the other parent.

Creating a Co-Parenting Team

As you have heard many times, there is no "I" in team. To create your co-parenting team, it's important to look at it from a neutral perspective in terms of strengths and weaknesses you both bring to the table. No one has the perfect co-parenting relationship, just as there is no perfect team; but the best teams make a plan for how they can best come together, emphasizing each person's strengths and how those strengths complement each other.

This exercise helps you understand where you work well together and where there might be more work to do. Think from your child's perspective, and attempt to understand through that lens what each parent brings to the co-parenting dynamic.

1. Describe how your child benefits from their relationship with each parent.

2. Where do you feel there are differences in how each of you parents?

3. In what way will you work well together?

4. Where will there be challenges?

_____

_____

_____

_____

_____

_____

_____

_____

Aligning Values in Co-Parenting

Circle three values you would like to instill in your children. There are also spaces to write your own values.

The importance
of family

Inner peace
and harmony

Volunteering and giving
back to the community

A healthy lifestyle

Creativity

Fun and adventure

Economic stability
and responsibility

Respect for self
and others

Strong cultural identity

Work ethic

Religious beliefs or
spirituality

Acceptance of various
lifestyles or gender/
sexual orientations

Planning for the future

Community activism

Integrity and honesty

_____

_____

Now, quickly—write down one way you and your co-parent can instill these values in your child, together. Take turns doing this!

Partner 1:

_____

_____

Partner 2:

_____

_____

THERESA AND MIGUEL

Theresa and Miguel met when they were in college and had a passionate relationship. Their lives together were filled with sex, drugs, and rock 'n' roll. Both came from dysfunctional homes and never learned healthy communication skills. Marriage and children only exacerbated the issues in their relationship. After having children, Theresa got sober and decided she wanted to be a different role model than her mother was for her.

Theresa started to suspect that Miguel's heavy substance use had crossed the line into addiction. Theresa got into therapy and started attending Al-Anon, a 12-step program for partners and family members of individuals with substance use disorder. She also took some parenting classes, recognizing that good parenting skills weren't modeled for her. As Theresa got healthier, she became more intolerant of Miguel's substance use, and their fighting escalated until, one night, it nearly turned into a physical altercation in front of the children. Theresa packed herself and her children up and left that night.

Fast-forward five years later. Theresa and Miguel are divorced, and both have happily remarried. Miguel went to rehab and maintained his sobriety in a 12-step program. Theresa recognized how important it was for her children to have a relationship with Miguel, despite their history, so she formed a cordial relationship with Miguel's wife. Theresa realized Miguel's style of parenting was looser, with fewer rules and responsibilities, but the children had a good relationship with him, so she was willing to embrace the idea that her kids were able to enjoy their time with their father. She focused on providing a good routine and structure in her own home. Miguel was able to recognize that the structure Theresa provided for the kids made them more responsible humans. Theresa and Miguel made a commitment not to speak poorly about each other in front of the kids and to come directly to each other if they disagreed. They also decided on an overall rewards and consequences system, even though they might parent differently in each home. The co-parenting scenario has matured to the point that all four parents are able to attend events for the children together and enjoy a cordial relationship that can even include taking pictures together.

How to Use This Workbook

You and your partner may agree on almost everything except about being in a relationship, or you may only be able to focus on your child's success. There may be more challenging co-parenting dynamics that arise as you take up this new chapter of your family's life, but this book will help prepare you for those obstacles. There is always room to grow, heal, and learn healthier ways of communicating. That being said, this book isn't designed to be a replacement for therapy for you or your children; rather, it is intended to be a complementary tool.

You will each be given an opportunity to heal yourself as you work through this book. As you heal, you will be better able to show up for your kids. Your kids will benefit from a stable, secure home environment that is also loving and nurturing. You will also be modeling healthy vulnerability for your kids. What a gift!

In most cases, children communicate through their behavior. When you are not present with them because you are dealing with grief, stress, or anxiety, they will sense it, and this will often show up as unwanted behavior. Kids are incredibly intuitive, and even if you think you are hiding your pain, they will still pick up on your energy. The more you are able to stay grounded and present with them, which will naturally occur as you heal yourself, the more their behavior will improve.

If you are attempting to co-parent with someone who has a severe untreated mental illness or active addiction, please consult with a therapist for additional help. Co-parenting with these individuals may not be possible, and you will need resources to help you deal with your specific situation. If you are dealing with domestic violence, please contact the domestic violence hotline at 800-799-SAFE (7233) or your local law enforcement agency immediately.

Make sure to complete the exercises as you both read through this book, since they give you an opportunity to reflect on your personal situation. Be honest with yourself as you read through the material, and take ownership for mistakes each of you may have made in the past. Remember to consider your co-parent's point of view while giving them the benefit of the doubt for their own foibles. You weren't handed an instruction manual on how to parent. Give yourself some grace, and congratulate yourself on taking this step toward becoming a better parent!

Strengths Each Person Brings to Co-Parenting

List five positive traits that you feel you bring to your parenting relationship with your child:

1. _____

2. _____

3. _____

4. _____

5. _____

List five positive traits that you feel your co-parent brings to their parenting relationship:

1. _____

2. _____

3. _____

4. _____

5. _____

Observe and acknowledge any resistance that comes up as you sit with this. What resistance did you experience?

_____

_____

_____

List five goals that both of you would like to achieve as you work toward a healthy co-parenting relationship:

1. _____

2. _____

3. _____

4. _____

5. _____

1. _____

2. _____

3. _____

4. _____

5. _____

POSITIVITY PAUSE

We love our children enough to take ownership of our mistakes and strive to understand each other's point of view. We are willing to acknowledge and work through our pain and negative feelings so we can heal and be better co-parents. We are motivated to do this work so we can be healthy role models for our children!

Chapter Takeaways

In order to have a successful co-parenting relationship where your child thrives beyond the breakup of your primary relationship, you must be willing to start a new chapter with your former partner. When you had children with them, you signed on for a parenting relationship for life. Although the romantic relationship ended, the family did not; it will just take on a different form. As you approach this complex situation, be mindful of the following:

1. Remember the importance of putting your child first as you form a co-parenting relationship.

2. Be open to creating a new co-parenting relationship with your former partner that's future-focused. Be willing to stop looking in the rearview mirror.

3. Work toward forming a joined and united team-based approach in your co-parenting relationship.

4. Embrace different parenting styles, and respect the bond each of you shares with your child.

5. Foster your child's secure attachment with each parent by speaking about the other parent in positive terms in front of the child.

What was your biggest lesson from this chapter?

_____

_____

_____

What insight did you gain about yourself that will help you work better with your co-parent as you move forward?

_____

_____

_____

Next Steps

- Notice if you are tempted to say something negative about your co-parent in front of your child. Take a deep breath and reframe it to something more positive.

- Throughout the week, make a concerted effort to notice what your co-parent is doing well, rather than focusing on what they are doing wrong. Journal about it.

- Notice the positive traits your child inherited from the other parent.

- Be specific about what your motivation is to create a team-based approach to parenting.

CHAPTER TWO

Developing a Co-Parenting Plan

Creating a co-parenting plan together will help you form a united, team-based approach. A good plan will incorporate a rewards and consequences system while being flexible enough to accommodate differing parenting styles. It also will include the understanding that your child may not have the language or ability to communicate verbally what they are feeling, so you both must consider how they might be communicating through their behavior. It's important for the parents to separate the behavior from the emotions and make it clear that unwanted behavior is an unhealthy way of expressing emotions. Both parents will need to be empathetic toward the emotions while normalizing and validating them. You both will need to become comfortable with your own vulnerability so you can be empathetic toward your child's emotional experience. You will also need to help your child come up with healthier ways of expressing their emotions while setting limits on unwanted behavior.

What Is a Co-Parenting Plan?

Children like certainty. They like to know what to expect. If they feel uncertain or anxious, they may have a hard time expressing it. To understand why communicating feelings is difficult for children, it's helpful to understand what is happening with their brains. A child's brain development continues until they reach their mid-20s. The more logical part of the brain, the prefrontal cortex, doesn't start developing until adolescence. This is the area where executive functioning occurs. As parents, your role is to help your child's executive functioning develop in a healthy way by providing good routine and structure in a loving and nurturing environment. A parenting plan, which is a written, mutually agreed-upon document that outlines the framework and boundaries that will be consistent among households, helps provide a structured, nurturing environment where your child's brain can become integrated and whole. This can be accomplished across two households if both co-parents are willing to work together.

In order to be productive when working with your co-parent, it's important for both of you to be aware that this is not a unilateral plan. It is crucial that both parents be committed and willing to enforce what they agree upon. If one person is acquiescing to the other person and feeling unheard, they will be less likely to enforce the plan. Some negotiating and a willingness to see each other's perspective is essential to the plan's success.

It Creates Consistency

A parenting plan will create consistency across households and help your child more gently acclimate to the new family dynamics. This is your opportunity to minimize the trauma of the change for them. Assuming you and your co-parent can agree on the major issues and create a plan to address them, your child can relax because they will know what to expect in each household. Once your child realizes that you and your co-parent are consistent and communicating about their care, they can focus on being a kid. Understanding the values and background that drive each person's parenting style will help you understand each other's perspective when you are unable to agree. In the early stages of this new dynamic, it may be more challenging to communicate effectively. If at any point the conversation becomes escalated, end it and come back to it when you are both feeling calm and able to be more productive.

It Establishes Routine

The best way to start crafting a parenting plan is by talking through your child's routine. This is the foundation on which you will build the rest of the plan. A routine helps all parties adapt to the new way of life. It also creates certainty for your child so they know what to expect, thus minimizing their stress. Consider what consistency is necessary and doable across homes, such as wake-up and bedtimes, or when you expect them to complete their school-work. You will also need to consider routines for regular activities that take place outside the home, such as who accompanies the child to extracurriculars or coordinates transportation. The younger the child, especially 10 years old and younger, the more consistent you both need to be with the routine. As the child gets older and into their teenage years, they can have more of a voice in what the routine looks like.

It Helps Resolve Potential Conflict

A solid co-parenting plan helps you anticipate and resolve any potential conflicts before they arise. Conflict is the biggest obstacle to forming a united front in co-parenting and causes the most stress for the child. By having the conversation proactively when you are both in a calm, logical place, you can think through how to handle challenging situations with your children, as well as with each other. Because the plan is mutually developed, both parties have their expectations set. Even when a conflict arises, parents will know they have already agreed upon their common goal and how to achieve it. Since both parties are on the same page about how to handle potential conflicts, you won't need to make decisions when emotions are high. You can both relax and automatically implement the plan when needed. It's important to include boundaries in this section of the plan, such as agreeing not to bait each other into an argument or taking a break when one of you is feeling emotionally overwhelmed. You can make an agreement to come back and discuss the topic at a later date.

It Sets Expectations

As you and your co-parent prepare to sit down together and start working on your parenting plan, it's important to set expectations. Establish an agenda for the conversation, as well as a timeline if more than one meeting is required. It's also helpful to discuss upfront what topics are off the table for discussion, such as the issues that ended your romantic relationship or any current relationships that either or both of you are involved in. The focus should be on your children.

In order to accomplish this, you both will need to set an intention to keep the conversation productive and incorporate some self-soothing techniques when either of you feels triggered. Be aware of what happens in your body when you feel triggered. Do you feel tightness in your chest, does your breathing get more shallow or more rapid, do you feel nauseous, do you get a headache, or does your throat tighten up? These physical sensations are your body's message to you that you need to self-soothe. Have an agreement that you will allow each other to step away and self-soothe if you need to do so.

It Helps with Major Decision-Making

During a child's lifespan, there are several major decisions that need to be made, and this is your opportunity to plan for those.

- How will decisions be made for education?

- How about religion?

- How will health-care decisions be made? (This is a such an important topic that it is included as its own section on page 32.)

- What about childcare and extracurricular activities?

- Who will pay for what?

There are many day-to-day decisions that need to be addressed, too:

- Will you discuss those decisions, or will they be made unilaterally by the parent who has custody of the child at the time?

- How will that decision be communicated to the other parent?

Think through the major decisions that you anticipate will apply to your child, and come up with a plan for how to handle them.

Goals for Your Co-Parenting Plan

Attempting to co-parent without a co-parenting plan will inevitably result in miscommunication, conflict, and frustration. Reviewing the areas discussed in this section, circle the areas in your co-parenting relationship that you feel could be addressed with a good co-parenting plan. Underneath the area(s) that you selected, give some context around why these are issues in your co-parenting relationship. You will be given specific guidance on these areas later in this book, but it's helpful to have a broad idea of what you would like to establish in your co-parenting plan.

Create Consistency

_____

_____

_____

_____

_____

Establish Routine

_____

_____

_____

_____

_____

Prevent and Resolve Potential Conflict

_____

_____

_____

_____

_____

Set Expectations

_____

_____

_____

_____

_____

Help with Major Decision-Making

_____

_____

_____

_____

_____

Self-Soothing Techniques

Assemble a plan to self-soothe in case you get triggered as you are meeting with your co-parent. Think about a time recently when you felt anxious or upset and were able to calm yourself down. What method did you use? Can it or some version of it be used to help you self-soothe, even if you need to take a time-out to implement it?

Choose from the following list, or write in some of your own:

- Listen to calming music.

- Do yoga stretches.

- Practice deep breathing: Slowly inhale while counting to 4, filling your lungs, hold for half a second, then slowly exhale while counting to 4 and, with your lungs empty, hold for half a second. Repeat.

- Call a nurturing, trusted friend who knows that your ultimate goal is to come up with a plan and who can help you stay calm.

_____

_____

_____

_____

_____

_____

_____

_____

_____

JESSICA AND TINA

Jessica loved children and always wanted to be a mom, but her partner, Tina, didn't feel she had strong maternal instincts. Tina loved Jessica, though, so she agreed when Jessica begged her to adopt a child together. They eventually adopted a four-year-old boy named Xavier. Being a mother brought out a controlling instinct in Jessica that Tina had not seen before. As her own maternal instincts were emerging, she didn't feel that her voice was heard or validated when it came to parenting. Though she did bond with Xavier, she was feeling more and more emotionally and physically disconnected from Jessica. Two years after adopting Xavier, Tina had an affair with an ex-girlfriend, Debbie, who she had reconnected with on social media. When Jessica found out about the affair, their breakup was messy. Tina decided to move out to prevent the two of them from fighting in front of Xavier.

Jessica, who felt abandoned after Tina moved out, was incredibly hurt by Tina's affair. She was also aware of how resentful she felt when Xavier was excited to be in Tina's custody. After taking some time to heal, Jessica was able to recognize that Tina and Xavier had created a bond that was uniquely different from the more nurturing bond she herself shared with him. Tina enjoyed throwing the ball and playing video games with Xavier. Jessica realized she could do those things with their son, but she didn't share Tina's passion for those activities. She reached out to Tina to arrange a time to sit down and discuss a parenting plan. While meeting with Tina, Jessica was mindful of when her thoughts were starting to venture to the affair, and after taking some deep breaths, she made an intentional effort to redirect her thoughts to Xavier and what was best for him. Tina shifted away from defensiveness and became more empathetic to Jessica's emotional experience when she observed how Jessica was no longer making baiting comments about their breakup. They agreed on a parenting plan and have both moved on with their lives.

What Goes in the Plan?

In this section, you will learn the nuts and bolts of what goes into a good parenting plan at a high level. If you aren't able to cover all of these areas in your first meeting, you can break this process up into two or three meetings. If you have a legal document, such as a separation agreement or divorce decree, in which some of these specifics are already outlined, feel free to skip to the sections that apply to you.

Communication Methods

This is where you both agree on what communication will look like as you embark on your new relationship as co-parents. How will you exchange information? Will you communicate over text, email, or phone? You might also determine that certain incidents elicit different types of communication. Perhaps you agree that you will mostly communicate over text but will call each other in the case of an emergency. Many co-parents find it helpful to email each other a synopsis of what happened while the child was in their custody. This is a proactive method of staying on the same page. You might also consider work schedules and which type of communication is appropriate during the workday. If communication was poor or cut off at the end of your romantic relationship, this is your opportunity to discuss how to communicate in a healthy way going forward.

Also consider how each parent will communicate with the child while the co-parent has custody. What time of day will be carved out for the child to communicate with the other parent, and what method of communication will they use? How frequently will they communicate with the other parent?

Rewards and Consequences System and Discipline Expectations

This section is where you can discuss a rewards and consequences system. It is very important that you both agree on the rewards and consequences you outline so you will be consistent across households. Consistency is key for making the system work fairly for your child.

Be clear about what action or behavior will elicit a reward or consequence. Be specific about what the reward or consequence will be for specific actions or behaviors. For example, if you promise to take your child shopping for new clothes if they agree to study for one hour every weekday this week, does this mean a new wardrobe or a couple of new shirts and pants? The same applies to consequences. Think about what is realistic. For example, let's say in a fit of anger you take away your child's phone for a month; how will you communicate with your child during that time? Perhaps a month is too long, and you end up giving your child's phone back early. Or your co-parent doesn't agree with that length of time and ends up giving the phone back early without discussing it with you, thus causing a break in your unified front. Agree in advance on what discipline is realistic and enforceable but doesn't leave the parents feeling like they are being punished as well.

Finances

In this section of the parenting plan, you will talk through how you want to handle expenses for your child. It is helpful if one or both of you can track these expenses in a spreadsheet over a couple of months so you have an idea of how much their expenses will be, at least for the time being. Consider a co-parenting app that enables you to track expenses, communicate, and share a calendar all in one place (see Resources, page 132). If you aren't an app person, one or both of you can track expenses in a shareable spreadsheet, such as Google Sheets, or simply email a spreadsheet to your co-parent once a month.

This section is also an opportunity talk through budgets for clothes, school activities, summer camps, and extracurricular activities so you are both on the same page about what is affordable and how much to spend.

Finally, talk through how money will be exchanged between you and your co-parent, such as whether one person gives the other a check, you use an app to transfer money, or you establish a joint account where money is held for your child's expenses.

Health-Care Decisions

Health care is a common area of disagreement for co-parents. Having a plan is incredibly helpful when you are dealing with your child's emotional and physical well-being.

Do your best to anticipate every possible scenario when it comes to your child's health, and talk through how you will communicate with your co-parent about managing decisions related to health care. You may find that you have different opinions on what constitutes an emergency or that one of you puts a higher priority on mental health. Talk through these issues and see if you can meet in the middle.

Consider who will schedule routine doctor, dentist, and/or mental health appointments and what notice should be provided to the other parent. Will you both attend these appointments, or will the parent who has custody of the child be responsible for taking the child to the appointment and reporting back to the other parent? If the child becomes sick or injured at school, who will pick them up, and how will the other parent be informed? If they are going to miss school because of being sick or hurt, who will take care of them?

Holidays, Vacations, and Special Events

To facilitate this discussion, it's helpful to have a list of holidays, important family dates, and upcoming vacations handy. It is important to remember that other special events will arise that are unforeseen, and these may pose a challenge because of negotiating uncomfortable feelings. Remember to have your child's best interests in mind when these challenges arise.

For holidays, will you alternate year to year, or will you split up the holiday so your child spends time with each of you on that day? When traveling, will you inform the other parent of the itinerary? How will both you and your child communicate with the other parent while traveling? How frequently and at what time of day will the co-parent speak with the child while they are on vacation with the other parent? Who will store the child's passport between trips, if one is required?

Special events can be wonderful opportunities to show your child that you are joined and united co-parents who can both attend an event or performance without conflict. You don't necessarily have to sit together. In fact, seeing you sitting together talking (or not talking) could feel awkward for the child, and they could be hyperaware of what is going on between you and not focused on their performance. Having said this, if you aren't able to relax, be present, and enjoy your child's performance with the other parent (and potentially their new partner) present, then perhaps consider a plan where the parent who has custody at that time takes the child to the event.

House Rules

There can be some flexibility in each house, but generally, you and your co-parent will need to talk through what is important to each of you in terms of house rules. Start the discussion by covering where your house rules will differ or match overall, especially with regard to chores, schedules, and homework. You may find that you have different opinions on how your child spends their time with each of you, but remember that some level of consistency is necessary to provide stability for your child, so try to find some overlap.

Break down the time your child spends in each home into specific activities, blocking off time for each activity. How much time is spent on chores? When will your child do their homework, and how much time is devoted to school-work overall? These are areas where the rewards system can be incorporated as a motivating tool for the child. It also teaches them to have a good work ethic and that hard work pays off! You might even consider keeping a chart somewhere centrally located in each home, like on the refrigerator, where you can list out chores and homework time, then check off when the tasks are completed so they can see how close they are to earning a reward. You might include fun pictures or gold stars so the child has a visual.

Living Arrangements and Schedule

Generally speaking, the younger the child is, the more consistent the schedule should be. As the child grows beyond age 10, you can become more flexible and allow them to have a voice in the schedule.

On which days and for how much time will the child be with each co-parent? For example, if you agree on a $^{50}/_{50}$ schedule, it might look like either one week on/one week off, or two days on/two days off/three days on, switching back and forth.

Once you have decided on a custody schedule and what that will look like, determine how the transition back and forth will be handled. Will you exchange custody at each other's homes or at a neutral location? How will you interact with each other? Even a simple "hi" to each other can go a long way in easing your child's stress.

If you need to change the schedule, how will you communicate this, and how much notice will you give each other? How quickly should the other party respond to the request? Do you need to confirm the change in writing?

When and How to Introduce New Partners

A perfectly amicable co-parenting relationship can unravel if introducing a new partner to the children is poorly handled. Bringing a new adult into the family can throw the whole system off-balance and create feelings of insecurity, anxiety, or fear for the co-parent. Usually, these feelings are connected to the idea that this new person, who they probably have never met, could be interacting with their child. Consider whether you would like the other parent to meet the new partner before you introduce them to the child. Think through the timing of when you would like to introduce a new partner to your child. After six months of exclusive dating? After a year? How long should the relationship be in existence before the new partner is allowed to stay overnight while the child is in that parent's custody? The timing is completely up to you and your co-parent, but it's important that you both agree. Once you have decided to introduce a new partner to your child, the best practice is that the person planning to introduce the new partner informs the other parent in some way so they aren't hearing about it from the child later. It's important to recognize that you aren't asking for permission. You simply are giving your co-parent the courtesy of a heads-up.

Start Prioritizing Topics for Your Co-Parenting Plan

From the following list, take turns checking three topics that you think are a priority to address in your first parenting plan meeting. Then, collaborate to decide which topics will be covered in the initial meeting.

☐ Communication Methods

☐ Rewards and Consequences System and Discipline Expectations

☐ Finances

☐ Health-Care Decisions

☐ Holidays, Vacations, and Special Events

☐ House Rules

☐ Living Arrangements and Schedule

☐ When and How to Introduce New Partners

How to Address the Initial Topics in Your Co-Parenting Plan

Each co-parent should do this exercise individually to prepare for the first meeting. Give a brief explanation for why the topics you agreed to cover in the first meeting need to be addressed, and then provide some ideas on how to address them.

Why they need to be addressed:

_____

_____

_____

_____

Potential solutions:

_____

_____

_____

_____

Creating a Plan

Now that you know what goes into the plan and what topics are priorities to address in your first meeting, it's time to start preparing for the discussion. This is also the time to think through strategies for self-soothing to stay emotionally regulated while meeting with your co-parent.

Start by creating an agenda for the first meeting. It's important for the first meeting to be successful so you both will feel motivated to continue. Don't bite off more than you can chew. Start by addressing the three topics you agreed on from page 35. It's helpful to put a mission statement at the top of your agenda, including your children's names, to keep you both focused. For example: *"We work collaboratively on this parenting plan with the mutual desire for the highest and best well-being of our children at the forefront of our minds. Julie, Jonah, and Justin thrive from our cordial and united co-parenting."* You can also include an intention to establish boundaries for the meeting, such as: *"This is the start of a new chapter as co-parents, and our discussion will be fact-based, solution-oriented, and future-focused."* Keep in mind that a parenting plan can change over time, but starting a plan now can lead to a successful co-parenting relationship long-term.

As you think through the agenda, notice any anxiety or resistance. What physical sensations are you feeling? Anticipate that these will magnify when you are in the presence of your co-parent. Journal about these thoughts and feelings so you can make sense of them. Now, gently redirect your thoughts. Think deeply about what is important to you and your child. Remember the ideal co-parenting situation you imagined (page 5)? Recall that vision, and then notice how you feel. Are you more excited and motivated? Hold on to that image of the ideal, and use it as your motivator to stay emotionally regulated during the meeting.

No More "My Way or the Highway"

Any good parenting plan will have some flexibility built into it. Being too rigid and unwilling to meet your co-parent halfway is not productive. Having said this, there are likely some expectations that you feel you must have in order to improve the relationship. Let's break these elements down into specifics that you want to include in the parenting plan to help you achieve your vision of ideal co-parenting. Which components are you flexible on, and which are must-haves? For example: *"I must have cordial, peaceful communication with my co-parent,"* **and** *"I'm willing to be flexible with bedtime to accommodate my co-parent's work schedule."*

Start Drafting a Parenting Plan

In this exercise, each of you will develop your own template for a co-parenting plan. Then, you will share it with the other parent, combining your individual ideas until you are able to agree. Here's an example.

> ## CO-PARENTING PLAN FOR THE [INSERT LAST NAME] FAMILY
>
> *We, (co-parent name) and (co-parent name), parents of (children's names), are entering into a shared parenting agreement in order to ensure our children's well-being and safeguard their future development. We both agree that we love our children and want what's best for them, regardless of how we feel about each other. We agree that the welfare for our children can best be achieved by mutual cooperation in parenting. We strive to provide a joined and united front in our parenting so our children can rest assured that their needs will be met. We will both provide a home environment in which our children feel loved and supported. We also understand that each of us wants what is best for our children, and we will keep that at the forefront of every interaction with each other and in every decision we make on behalf of our children.*

Now, take a moment to write down your own co-parenting plan on a separate sheet of paper. Share that with your co-parent, and talk about your similarities and differences. Then, record your child's information in the following table.

CHILDREN

NAME	DATE OF BIRTH	SSN

POSITIVITY PAUSE

We acknowledge that we are human and will likely be triggered when we meet with each other to discuss our parenting plan. We are open-minded and willing to attempt to self-soothe so we can keep our conversation productive. We are motivated to implement this strategy so our children can flourish going forward.

Chapter Takeaways

You are starting to see a strategy emerge on how to form a successful co-parenting relationship with your former partner. You might also be aware that, while forming a parenting plan may be challenging, it won't be a futile effort. Your child will be able to relax and focus on being a child when you have a plan for a joined and united co-parenting relationship. In addition, both of you can relax knowing you've thought through and planned for every possible scenario when you were both operating from the logical part of your brain, rather than trying to make an impulsive decision in the moment when feelings are heightened. In addition, you will benefit from learning how to self-soothe when you are feeling anxious or dealing with potential conflict, which will serve you well in all of your relationships.

The lessons from this chapter include:

1. How to create a parenting plan and what elements to include.

2. The importance of taking a collaborative approach where you both meet in the middle, versus a unilateral approach.

3. Acknowledging and owning your triggers.

4. Incorporating self-soothing strategies.

5. Using the vision of an ideal co-parenting relationship as your motivator to proceed.

What are some of your takeaways from this chapter?

_____

_____

_____

_____

What insight did you gain about yourself that you can use going forward?

_____

_____

_____

_____

Next Steps

Don't delay. Act now to create a parenting plan while you are feeling motivated. Early intervention is key!

- Arrange a time and place for your first parenting plan meeting, and send out a calendar invite to your co-parent to confirm.

- Formulate the agenda for the first meeting.

- Create a list of potential triggers and self-soothing exercises that you can implement if you start to feel triggered. Begin putting some of those exercises into practice now.

- Remind yourself that the plan can change over time, but you need to start somewhere!

CHAPTER THREE

Handling Communication and Conflict

n this chapter, we will cover communication in more depth, including unhealthy styles of communication and their healthier counterparts. Unhealthy ways of communicating are passed down from generation to generation. As co-parents, this is your opportunity to learn a healthier way of relating to each other and to other important people in your life. It starts with you being honest with yourself about how you communicate—good, bad, and ugly—and being willing to change any unhealthy patterns. There are strategies you can implement to change the dynamic if you are willing to give them a try.

Communication's Role

Your ability to communicate your feelings and needs to each other in a healthy and balanced way will have a big impact on the quality of your co-parenting relationship and, in turn, how well your child will acclimate to the new dynamic. It may be tempting to not communicate at all with your co-parent because you still harbor negative feelings toward each other. However, your child will sense your animosity, and it will cause them stress and put them in the middle of your tension. As you and your co-parent start to consider your new relationship, think about your boundaries. Boundaries are established through communication and are crucial to any successful co-parenting relationship. In order to communicate with each other effectively, you must have an understanding of your personal style of communicating. This is the first step toward making changes.

Let's take a look at the four types of communication:

Passive: Difficulty expressing feelings and needs, poor boundaries, trouble saying no

Aggressive: Speaking in a loud, intense, dominating way; blaming, intimidating, name-calling, mocking, belittling

Passive-Aggressive: Giving the cold shoulder, talking behind someone's back, eye-rolling, retreating from a discussion about conflict, using sarcasm, spreading rumors

Assertive: Owning and communicating one's feelings and needs while considering the needs of others; seeing another's perspective even if you don't agree with it; validating another's feelings; using "I" language and speaking only from your own experience

When someone has a passive style of communicating, they typically carry resentment because of their poor boundaries and inability to say no. Passive communicators often have a difficult time advocating for themselves and asking to have their needs met. This can lead to a passive-aggressive way of expressing the resentment. Often, a person will become more passive when their co-parent is more aggressive. The aggressive party will tend to be the one to "pursue" in times of conflict. This can come across as verbal attacks in the form of contempt, criticism, mocking, or belittling, thus causing the more passive person to feel emotionally overwhelmed and more likely to "retreat." Retreating usually comes in the form of stonewalling, giving the cold shoulder, checking out of the conversation, or walking away. When this happens, the pursuer's anxiety increases and they pursue more, causing more distancing from the other party. This is referred to as a *pursuer/distancer dynamic*.

With these unhealthy communication styles, there tends to be perpetual unresolved conflict and a never-ending self-sustaining feedback loop of the same fights over and over again. When co-parents get locked in this endless loop, communication can sometimes come to a halt. Co-parents may stop attempting to cooperate and begin parenting in "silos" with minimal communication, a concept known as *parallel parenting*. This dynamic can create a negative experience for the child, who can feel caught in the middle or conflicted about where to put their loyalty.

You can change these negative communication styles if you are willing to own your role in the communication breakdown. These styles involve unhealthy defense mechanisms, usually learned in childhood, that aren't serving the co-parenting relationship. The remedy is to become more assertive in how you communicate with each other. Keeping your partner's feelings and needs at the forefront of your communication, while being willing to see and understand each other's perspective even if you don't agree, will help you change the dynamic. Validating each other when you are able to will help you stay emotionally regulated so the conversation remains productive.

Learning Your Style of Communication

Here are some constructive and destructive passive and active communication patterns. Being honest with yourself, circle which ones apply to you:

	PASSIVE	ACTIVE
DESTRUCTIVE (PASSIVE, AGGRESSIVE, OR PASSIVE-AGGRESSIVE) STYLES	Avoiding Yielding Hiding emotions Self-criticizing Saying yes when you want to say no Having poor boundaries	Winning at all costs Displaying anger Demeaning others Retaliating Criticizing Using sarcasm
CONSTRUCTIVE (ASSERTIVE) STYLES	Reflective thinking Delaying responding until more logical Adapting	Perspective-taking Creating solutions Expressing emotions Reaching out Validating feelings

Once you have selected the style(s) that you identify with the most, think about how your style of communicating has an impact on your relationships. Describe it here:

_____

_____

_____

_____

_____

_____

_____

_____

As you think through your life and how your communication style developed, what are you learning about yourself?

_____

_____

_____

_____

_____

_____

_____

_____

Connecting with Your Existing Assertive Communication Skills

Recall a time when you were able to resolve a conflict with someone in your life using assertive communication skills. Describe it here:

_____

_____

_____

_____

_____

How were you able to keep yourself calm and emotionally regulated as you worked through this conflict? Did you take a break to collect your thoughts, write your thoughts down before communicating them, slow yourself down so you could think through your responses, or use another method?

_____

_____

_____

_____

_____

Now, think about a recent disagreement you had with your co-parent. How could this have been handled more assertively using these same skills?

_____

_____

_____

_____

_____

Thinking from your child's perspective, how will they benefit from your efforts to be more assertive in your communication style with each other?

_____

_____

_____

_____

_____

Healthy and Productive Communication

You may have had trouble identifying poor communication patterns in your previous relationship, but as you establish your new co-parenting relationship, you both now have the opportunity to employ positive communication techniques. This will pay off in dividends for the emotional health of your child. As stated previously, as long as you recognize the unhealthy pattern and take ownership of your role in it, there is hope. Staying rooted in uncommunicated emotions while blaming the other person will not improve the situation. Fostering healthy communication patterns can help the co-parenting relationship and keep the focus where it should be: on your child. They will be free to be a kid instead of worrying about how their needs will be met. They won't have to feel the stress of communicating as a go-between. Imagine how liberating that will be for them!

To communicate more assertively, you must be willing to own and express your feelings, which feels scary when there is no guarantee your co-parent will meet you there. Hostility and anger serve a purpose: they protect you from having to feel vulnerable. Unfortunately, when you both stay locked in anger and hostility, there is no opportunity to open a door to a healthier way of co-parenting your child. Being more assertive in your approach makes it safer to communicate with each other, which in turn allows you to each be more flexible and adaptive in creating solutions for your child.

When co-parents are locked in the negative feedback loop (see page 54), at least one person must be willing to take the first step toward change in order to break the cycle. If one person adopts a healthier, more productive approach, the other person will likely respond.

If you both feel that communicating face-to-face or over the phone in this way is going to be too challenging at first, consider trying it out in email. Communicating in written form will give you both time to think through what you want to say to each other. It also allows for space to process your feelings so you can respond in a more productive way. If you need to discuss something in person and doing it over email isn't possible, bring a pen and notepad to take notes as you speak. The act of writing helps you stay grounded and logical as you communicate with each other. Remember to hit the pause button and take a break if you sense the negative cycle starting again. Give each other grace as you learn to navigate this new way of relating.

Exercising Your Assertive Communication Muscle

Looking at this example of unhealthy communication, you can see how emotion travels with words:

"You never ask me when I'll be free to talk to Beth when she's in your custody. You are so selfish! All you care about is yourself! I've been working my ass off so I can pay child support, and all you do is sit around NOT working and watching TV. You're so lazy! You obviously don't give a crap whether Beth has a relationship with her father."

Typically, when one feels attacked, they may get defensive:

"You know I am on the committee for Beth's play! Not to mention all the running around I do combined with other responsibilities I have to take care of since you work all the time! It's not my problem if you call right in the middle of bath and bedtime!"

An example of the first statement using assertive communication skills could look like:

"I know things can get crazy with Beth's bath and bedtime. I have been working longer hours trying to get a project done at work, and I really need to hear her voice at the end of the day. Would it be possible for us to work together to make sure she's available when I call?"

A healthier response could be:

"I'm so sorry, I've been overwhelmed with the play committee and other responsibilities, and our nighttime routine has gotten off-kilter. I know how much I appreciate you making sure Beth is available to talk to me when she's in your care. I promise to make sure she's free at 7:00 to speak to you. Does that work?"

Changing the Negative Feedback Loop

Now you know which communication style applies to each of you and how these styles can manifest in a pursuer/distancer dynamic. Describe a recent specific example of when one of you pursued and one of you distanced. For this exercise, focus more on what action you took as a pursuer or distancer and less on what was said in the conflict. Be sure to take responsibility for your role in the dynamic.

Pursuer:

_____

_____

_____

_____

_____

_____

_____

Distancer:

_____

_____

_____

_____

_____

_____

_____

When situations like this happen, it's best for the pursuer to resist their urge to pursue and allow the distancer to distance so they can have the time and space to process their emotions. In turn, the distancer needs to come back around and talk to the pursuer when they are ready and not sweep the issue under the rug. Think through the example again, considering how it could have played out differently if both of you had been given the time and space to process your feelings before coming back together using a more assertive approach. Describe it here:

_____

_____

_____

_____

_____

_____

_____

VICTORIA AND NASSIR

Victoria and Nassir met at a karaoke bar one night while Nassir was on leave from the military. They felt an instant attraction to each other, and Victoria loved how Nassir was so self-disciplined and motivated. She had a history of boyfriends who couldn't keep a job or pay their bills, and she always felt like their parent. Eighteen months later, they married and quickly had three children whom they initially called Mary, Elizabeth, and Lucas. Lucas was assigned male at birth but eventually came out as transgender and adopted the name Lucy.

From a very young age, Lucy wanted to play dolls with her sisters and was not interested in sports. Nassir had a hard time relating to Lucy and became angry toward her. Victoria felt she was constantly defending their child. Nassir had a strong reaction when, at 14 years old, Lucy came out as transgender. Fearful that Nassir's reaction could be harmful to Lucy, Victoria asked for a divorce, but, when Lucy assured her that she still wanted to have a relationship with her dad, she reached out to a therapist for help. As they transitioned to co-parents, Victoria and Nassir still argued over Lucy and her gender identity. In her work with the therapist, Victoria was able to realize that Nassir loved his daughter and always tried to show up for her, but his fear was getting in the way. She recognized that he felt lost and confused about how to relate to Lucy. She even acknowledged that Nassir was grieving the loss of the son he thought he was going to have when Lucy was born. Victoria acknowledged that she had become overprotective of her daughter, which kept her locked in anger and hostility and caused her to be critical and contemptuous toward Nassir.

In session one day, Victoria wrote out the dialogue for an email she planned to send to Nassir using a more assertive approach. She was essentially extending an olive branch to Nassir with no assurance he would grab it. Much to her surprise, Nassir responded well and admitted that he felt totally out of his element when trying to parent Lucy. Now that Victoria was providing a safe place for him to express his feelings without fear of harming Lucy, Nassir felt heard and validated. He ultimately decided to join a support group for men with transgender children. This not only gave him the emotional support he needed, but also helped him develop strategies for how to strengthen his relationship with Lucy.

Resolving Conflict

Even in the healthiest relationships, conflict occurs. For co-parents, the risk for conflict is higher because emotions are still raw. This can complicate matters as you both try to acclimate to the new co-parenting relationship. In some cases, there is so much contempt that conflict is all that exists between you. Only respond to triggering or negative communication from a nonemotional place, and only do this when a response is necessary. Don't take the bait; keep your tone neutral and use respect and kindness.

Try changing your perspective. When you think of your co-parenting relationship as a business relationship, it's easier to separate your emotions from the business of co-parenting. Imagine that your co-parent is a business partner who you have to work with to keep the business successful. Imagining your relationship through this lens, think about some high-conflict communication you have shared in the past. Would what you said to each other be acceptable in a business relationship? It's incredibly important for each of you to agree that you will prioritize trust and cooperation, as you would in a business relationship, to head off any potential conflicts.

Don't Take the Bait! Keeping Written Communication Productive

Let's take a look at another example of a baiting comment: *"I have told you a million times you cannot take our children to your office events because, even though you deny it, I know you had an affair with your boss. I will not have our children exposed to your philandering. My answer is no, you cannot take them during my custody time."*

It would be inappropriate to respond to this with emotion, defensiveness, or expressing your opinion. Not only could it escalate, but it could turn into a tit for tat that leads nowhere. Keep your response fact-based and friendly: *"Thank you for responding to my request to take the children to my co-worker's birthday party. In case I neglected to mention it previously, the party will be between 4:00 and 8:00 on Saturday, and about 10 co-workers from my department and their children, approximately six boys and girls, are invited, some of whom our children have met and enjoyed playing with. There will be no managers in attendance. My hope is that my co-workers who haven't met the kids will have the opportunity to do so at the party. Please let me know by 5:00 tomorrow if you are willing to reconsider. Thank you!"*

Using the techniques you have learned so far, write out a response to a communication you received recently that included a baiting comment:

_____

_____

_____

_____

Proactively Addressing Potential Conflict

The following table lists some common co-parenting conflicts and frequently used solutions.

Not honoring drop-off and pick-up times (frequently late)	Sometimes "life" happens, and people are late. Communicate how this affects the child's routine and structure while reminding your co-parent about the agreed upon schedule. If the other parent is always late, you may have to accept it and make accommodations.
Inability to talk to the child while in the other parent's custody	Make a commitment to each other that the child and the phone will be made available at a designated window of time. If something comes up, communicate this to the other parent, preferably in advance, to arrange an alternative time.
Putting the child in the middle when there is conflict	Take a break, think about the issue from the child's perspective, and reframe.
Jealousy of the other parent's time with the child (could lead to passive-aggressive behavior)	Think about how the child is benefiting from this positive experience with the other parent. Redirect your thoughts to focus on how you can provide a uniquely positive experience when the child is with you.
Excessive worrying about the child when they are with the other parent	Has something happened in the past that is causing your worry now? Are your fears related to what you know your child to be doing at this time? Find a way to self-soothe, to both assess the situation calmly and act effectively if there is cause to worry.
Learning about your co-parent's new romantic partner from the children	Give your co-parent a heads-up when you are about to introduce your new mate to the children. Remember, you aren't asking for permission. Just a quick text or email so they are hearing it from you, not your child.

After reading and considering this table, what would you consider to be the most common conflict between you and your co-parent? If there is more than one, describe the most pressing issue.

_____

_____

_____

Without pointing fingers, brainstorm a solution to this conflict and share it with your co-parent.

_____

_____

_____

_____

_____

_____

_____

_____

_____

_____

_____

_____

_____

_____

_____

DEALING WITH A TOXIC EX

If you or your ex has a high-conflict personality, mental illness may be playing a role in the form of a personality disorder (such as borderline personality disorder or narcissistic personality disorder). In some cases, you or your ex might be experiencing active alcoholism or addiction. Perhaps there was abuse in the relationship. Any of these issues will likely make direct communication with the other parent impossible.

For a high-conflict personality, there is a "supply" that comes from their partner taking the bait, and they will continue to try to bait others into an argument. You will need to cut off the supply. You may need to resort to strictly written communication using the techniques outlined in this chapter or hire a parent coordinator to facilitate communication. If you have to engage with the other parent face-to-face, be sure to work with a therapist to develop a safety plan so you have protection and can safely exit the interaction. In these cases, parallel parenting may be the better alternative for your child. In parallel parenting, the parents have extremely limited contact with each other and parent independently. This dynamic might be the only way to avoid exposing your child to perpetual conflict. Sometimes, when setting boundaries and communicating in this way, the other party will become more escalated at first. Individuals with personality disorders generally don't like boundaries because they lose a sense of control. Over time, hopefully, they will adjust if you continue to cut off the supply and enforce boundaries. If for any reason you feel concerned for your or your child's safety, contact the domestic violence hotline 800-799 SAFE (7233) or your local law enforcement agency immediately.

Chapter Takeaways

Understanding each of your roles in the self-sustaining feedback loop is the first step to making changes. Having healthier communication will open up the possibility of a better co-parenting relationship where your child benefits. Any conflict that existed in the previous relationship dynamic will likely remain unless you change how you communicate. This is how you establish boundaries: by anticipating potential conflict and proactively making a plan to eliminate the conflict. Imagine how much more peace you each will have in your life if you don't have conflict with your co-parent. Now, imagine how much better this will be for your child. The change starts by acknowledging whether your communication style is aggressive, passive, or passive-aggressive.

1. Shift to more assertive communication with each other.

2. Communicate your feelings and needs using "I" language while putting your child first.

3. Treat each other like business partners.

4. Anticipate and resolve potential conflicts.

Which of the unhealthy communication styles can you own? Now, think about your own childhood to understand where that style may have developed:

_____

_____

_____

Think about a challenging business relationship or relationship with a co-worker that you were able to improve by being more assertive. Describe it here:

_____

_____

_____

Next Steps

- Keep a picture of your child handy to reflect on when you communicate with your co-parent as motivation to be more assertive in your communication style.

- Notice if you are using an unhealthy style of communicating in your other relationships with friends, family, or co-workers. Practice being more assertive.

- If you are locked in hostility and anger, imagine how much peace you could have in your life if you no longer had to hold on to those negative feelings. What other areas of your life would improve as well?

- Start using the BIFF technique when communicating with your co-parent. Try it out in written communication first until you develop this skill.

- If you have a toxic ex, you may have only just recognized that you may be giving them a "supply." Without getting defensive, ask a trusted friend to honestly share what they have observed.

PART TWO

Healing and Thriving

CHAPTER FOUR

Helping Your Child Thrive

This chapter covers helping your child acclimate to the new family dynamic and develop coping skills that will serve them well into adulthood. You'll learn how to compartmentalize feelings associated with your co-parent so you can help your child better cope. You will also read about strategies for fostering open and honest communication with your child so they have a safe place to express their emotions. This section also provides you with interventions to help empower your child to make the mind/body connection, learn to regulate their nervous system, and develop strength-based coping skills that feel authentic to them.

Look Inward First

By now, you both can see why it's so important to put your child first in a successful co-parenting relationship. Co-parents will need to put their anger, hurt, resentment, and other negative feelings on the back burner in the early stages of forming their new dynamic. This does not mean those feelings should be stuffed down, swallowed, or ignored; it just means that you both will need to work toward not allowing those feelings to drive your co-parenting relationship. This can be very difficult when you might be concerned that those feelings are creating an obstacle to helping your child thrive. If you feel you need immediate intervention to manage your emotional state so you can better parent your child, flip to chapter 6 (page 109) and learn how to start your healing journey. You can also seek professional help by consulting with a therapist. It's important to accept that you may not be operating as your best self, and that you need to take steps to deal with your emotions. Treat yourself with compassion as you move through this transition. As you heal yourself, you will be better able to offer a safe place where your child can process their own emotions.

Negative Emotions as an Obstacle to Helping Your Child Thrive

Sometimes it can be hard to identify exactly what you are feeling. Take a look at the following list of emotions. Circle any you are experiencing that are creating an obstacle to you prioritizing your child's security and well-being.

Confused	Guilty	Irritable
Incompetent	Sad	Lonely
Worthless	Embarrassed	Deceived
Obsessed	Foolish	Abandoned
Jealous	Hopeless	Betrayed
Depressed	Hurt	
Angry	Ashamed	

It's normal to feel emotions when dealing with a breakup, and it is very common to stuff the feelings down and neglect your self-care as you are trying to meet your child's needs. As you reflect on your negative emotions, journal about how you might have neglected your own self-care. Include ways that you used to take care of yourself that have fallen by the wayside.

_____

_____

_____

_____

Create a Safe and Loving Environment

Creating a safe, loving, nurturing environment with good routine and consistency within the co-parenting structure is the ideal way to help your child through the upheaval that comes with a change to the family unit. When your child is feeling negative emotions, it's important that you don't try to "fix" it for them. This is your opportunity to show empathy by sitting with them and their emotions. It is so important for you to be in a stable, grounded place so you can stay present with your child in their emotional process.

In creating a parenting plan, you laid the framework for what the routine and structure will look like based on your unique situation. Now, it's time to plan for how to help your child manage their emotions that accompany this change.

In general, the younger the child, the more egocentric they tend to be. Up until they are six years old, children tend to only think about how circumstances impact their own lives. They aren't as concerned about the feelings or needs of those around them. They also like to know what to expect. If they don't have certainty, they will create scary stories in their heads that are not based in fact, and this will cause them to become anxious. Understanding this can help you see and speak from their perspective when communicating with them.

Now that you have a parenting plan in place, you can not only assure your child of what will remain the same for them, but also help prepare them for the changes that are to come. Children sometimes have difficulty expressing what they are feeling, so try utilizing play or arts and crafts to help them express their emotions. Reading with your child can make them feel safe, loved, and able to express themselves. Reading stories together about expressing emotions and then asking your child if they relate to the story using feeling words can be incredibly helpful.

As your child ages, they will become more aware of the feelings and needs of others but still may have difficulty expressing what they are feeling. Over the age of six and into the teenage years, be aware of whether your child is feeling responsible for your feelings and suppressing their own. Help them understand that you are responsible for your own feelings, and assure them that all they need to do is focus on being a kid.

In some cases, you might not have confidence that your co-parent is going to offer the same safe, nurturing environment. Assuming your child's physical safety isn't in danger when they are with the other parent, if you continue to provide stability for the child, it can help offset any inconsistencies that might be happening in the other home. If you have attempted to assertively communicate your concerns with your co-parent and they aren't willing to make changes, you may need to accept this reality. However, you can work hard to empower your child to set their own boundaries and know what is and isn't appropriate behavior. Worrying or obsessing about what is happening in the other home only distracts you from providing a safe, nurturing environment in your own home.

Methods to Create a Safe and Loving Environment

Following are methods to create a safe, nurturing environment for your child. Check off three you can implement right now:

☐ Read a book together at bedtime.

☐ Using crayons, draw a picture of the family. Notice any emotions being expressed, even through the use of color, and reflect them back to your child.

☐ Carve out expressive arts time where you do arts and crafts with your child. Make this time consistent and be sure to follow through. Notice if they are expressing emotions through their art.

☐ Get a sand tray with plastic toys that the child can use to create imaginary scenes to express their emotions.

☐ Print out an image from the internet with faces or emojis showing various emotions. Ask your child to indicate which one resonates with them to help them express an emotion.

☐ Have your child pick out a cool diary, buy it for them, and give them topics to journal about.

☐ Make a regular "date" with your child where they choose the activity you will do together. Let them determine what you discuss without directing them to a certain topic.

☐ Seek the help of a pediatric therapist.

An Empathetic Approach to Bad Behavior

Think about a recent time when your child was expressing emotion or when the emotion was showing up in their behavior. Describe it here:

_____

_____

_____

Describe how you responded to the behavior:

_____

_____

_____

After reflecting on this situation and standing in your child's shoes, what do you think they might have been feeling?

_____

_____

_____

Does this change your opinion of how you responded? If so, how could you have handled this situation more empathetically?

_____

_____

_____

AISHA AND RAYNIER

Aisha and Raynier had an unintended pregnancy after three months of dating. They tried to live together but soon realized they weren't compatible. Aisha, who was extroverted, social, and loved to travel, acknowledged from the beginning that she was selfish and never planned to be a parent. Raynier was more of a shy and introverted homebody. They agreed that Raynier would have primary custody of William, their son, with Aisha seeing William every other weekend and one night a week.

True to her word, Aisha was clearly not up for the responsibilities that came with being a mother and was inconsistent about her time with William. Raynier became frustrated as he saw how William suffered emotionally when Aisha didn't show up for her custody time with their son. Every time he confronted Aisha about it, she became defensive and they ended up fighting. In his work with his therapist, Raynier was able to accept that not all adults are meant to be parents and that Aisha was doing the best she could, considering she never wanted to be a mother. William loved sports, especially baseball, so Raynier carved out a couple of hours each week for them to throw the ball together or practice hitting at a local batting cage. Raynier always made sure dinner was served at the same time and created a rule of no TVs, phones, or tablets so there were no distractions during meals. Raynier encouraged William to talk about anything he wanted to while they ate. Sometimes, they didn't talk at all but would sit quietly together through the meal.

Over time, William felt safer sharing what he was feeling, and Raynier became more skilled at resisting his urge to "fix it" and instead learned to just sit with William as he expressed himself. Raynier learned when to be quiet and let William talk and when to reflect and validate his feelings. The more William expressed his feelings, the more he thrived. He was making friends at school and became more involved in extracurricular activities. As William got older, he learned not to expect more from his mother than she was able to give. He was able to enjoy his time with her while being grateful that he had such a close relationship with his father.

Foster Open Communication

When their children are feeling pain, parents often want to do everything they can to rescue them from feeling negative emotions. This urge can be particularly acute when a parent sees a negative situation on the horizon and wants to prevent a bad outcome for their child. This can create anxiety for the parent, and they will try to "fix it" for their child so that they, the parent, don't have to feel anxious anymore. When a parent is in "fix it" mode, from the child's perspective it can seem as if the parent is trying to force advice on them, control what the child is feeling, or, worse, shame the child for what they are feeling. In some cases, the child may feel they don't have a right to feel this way. Sometimes, the child will sense the parent's anxiety when they share and shut down altogether, because they don't want to cause the parent stress. The parent may have perfectly innocent intentions and feel they are helping the child, when in fact they are only making the child feel worse and as though they need to bury their emotions. This environment does not foster open and healthy communication. In most cases, the parent doesn't have the tools needed to create an environment for open and honest communication with their child.

People experience emotions in the mind and body simultaneously. When you observe your child going through an emotional experience, what thoughts are you having about that experience? Are you making negative predictions about an unknown future, or are you dwelling on regrets from the past that you can't change? Perhaps you are creating a story about what your child is experiencing that isn't based in fact, or you're excessively worrying about your child's thoughts, feelings, behaviors, actions, or decisions. These are referred to as *cognitive distortions*, and usually there are physical sensations that go along with them. A few examples include tearfulness, reduced appetite, poor sleep, nausea, tension throughout the body, tightness in the chest, or rapid, shallow breathing. Your physical experience is completely unique to you, but you will need to build awareness around it so you can self-soothe and be present with your child while they are experiencing their own cognitive distortions and accompanying physical sensations. Your child needs you to be present and emotionally available in order to feel safe being vulnerable with you.

Once you are able to self-soothe and become more present with your child, you will be better equipped to reflect back what they are feeling and empathize, even if you don't understand or agree with what they are feeling, without trying to fix it for them. It's common to feel like you need to provide solutions when your child is sharing their negative feelings, and in some cases this may be appropriate, but not before empathizing with your child. Empathy is an often-missed step in communication that is crucial for making sure your child feels heard and understood. Often, parents will try to provide solutions too soon in their eagerness to help, which is what happens when a parent goes into "fix it" mode. Empathy helps normalize and validate the child's feelings so they don't feel alone in their experience. It also fosters a strong emotional bond between parent and child. This is where the healing occurs.

Reprogramming Your Desire to Fix It

Think of a recent time when your child attempted to share their feelings with you and you went into "fix it" mode. Describe it here:

_____

_____

_____

_____

_____

_____

_____

_____

What were some of the cognitive distortions that were spinning around in your head (for example: regrets about the past, negative predictions about the future, story-making, or intrusive or repetitive thoughts about your child's thoughts, feelings, behaviors, or actions)? Write about them here:

_____

_____

_____

_____

_____

_____

_____

_____

Making the Mind and Body Connection

When you sit with cognitive distortions, scan your body. What are you feeling? Select from this list or write in your own:

☐ Tightness in chest

☐ Poor focus

☐ Rapid breathing

☐ Poor sleep

☐ Headache

☐ Reduced or increased appetite

☐ Stomachache

_____

_____

Reflecting on the exercise on page 69, how can you self-soothe and bring yourself back into the present so you can empathize with your child?

_____

_____

_____

Develop Healthy Coping Skills

According to an article published by VeryWellFamily.com, there are two types of coping skills: emotion-focused and problem-focused.

Emotion-focused coping skills are designed to help the child express their feelings and self-soothe when their head is spinning with cognitive distortions. This enables them to revisit the issue at hand later, when they are feeling more logical and better able to challenge their cognitive distortions.

Problem-focused coping skills involve helping the child come up with a solution in a situation that feels out of their control. Sometimes there is an action the child can take to change the situation that they are not yet aware of.

As you are helping your child develop emotion-focused coping skills, think about the hobbies and interests they naturally gravitate toward. Notice where they display strong aptitude, such as being musically inclined or artistically talented. Maybe they love sports or enjoy creating imaginary worlds. Notice if they are naturally introverted or extroverted. Having a good sense of your child's makeup and interests can help in developing a strength-based approach to their coping mechanisms. People tend to be more consistent with using healthy coping mechanisms if they feel authentic.

Helping your child develop problem-solving coping skills involves helping them come up with their own solutions to a problem. As stressed previously, don't jump to this step too soon or try to find the solution for them. Give your child a chance to express how they are feeling before you try to help them.

In general, when kids don't have healthy coping skills, they may act out in unhealthy ways. In younger kids, negative emotions will often show up as unwanted behavior. As kids grow into teenagers, you may see these emotions show up as avoidance, which could manifest as addiction. The teenager uses the addiction to distract themselves from feeling the negative emotions. Addictions can come in the form of alcohol and substances but can also show up with food, shopping, or other compulsive behaviors. This is an opportunity to use the change in the family dynamic in a positive way for your kids. They are essentially learning how to communicate their feelings and needs in a healthy and balanced way while learning how to self-soothe and cope with life challenges.

Helping Your Child Develop Coping Skills

Which of the following exercises would be effective in developing problem- or emotion-focused coping skills for your child?

Emotion-focused skills:

☐ Practicing deep breathing exercises

☐ Developing a meditation practice

☐ Doing yoga stretches

☐ Composing and/or performing a song to express their feelings

☐ Writing poetry

☐ Painting or drawing their feelings

☐ Playing video games that are designed to help develop coping skills (see Resources, page 132)

☐ Playing their favorite sport and "leaving it all on the field"

☐ Exercising or dancing

☐ Joining a support group where they can connect with peers who are dealing with the same experience

☐ Creating a "scene" with their dolls or toys to express their emotions

Write in some exercises that aren't represented here:

☐ _____

☐ _____

☐ _____

Problem-focused skills:

☐ Making a list of who they can ask for help (and have the child choose who they will ask)

☐ Creating a pros and cons list for each possible solution

☐ Listing out possible solutions and tuning in to their intuition to decide which one feels best

Write in some exercises that aren't represented here:

☐ _____

☐ _____

☐ _____

Helping Your Child Develop Mindfulness

Activities that focus on mindfulness help your child stay present in their day-to-day life. Being in nature has a grounding effect that can feel calming. Create a fun exercise with your child to help develop mindfulness while being in nature.

1. The adventure should encourage sensory experiences, like touching passing trees, smelling rain, or listening to faraway birds.

2. Try to focus on one sense at a time and take in all the little details.

3. Keep track of the smells you're picking up on. Are they the scents of the earth, the trees, the flowers?

4. Notice any sensations. Are you feeling anything against your skin? A breeze or the warmth of the sun? Stick your tongue out—do you taste anything?

5. Run through each of your senses with your child to see what they are experiencing.

6. Don't speak, just be present with each sense; when you get back to your car or home, talk about what you both noticed.

POSITIVITY PAUSE

We accept that we are human and that this change is difficult for both of us, as well as our child. We will do our best to compartmentalize our negative feelings for each other while healing ourselves so we can foster healthier communication and provide a safe, loving, and nurturing environment for our child. We acknowledge that learning how to cope now will have a long-lasting impact on how our child navigates difficult situations throughout their life.

Chapter Takeaways

Making the changes suggested in this chapter will be difficult, but the payoff will be great for your child. As you both help your child cope, you each will also be learning how to cope—so it's a win-win. As you embark on your own unique, individualized healing journey, you will each create opportunities for a closer emotional connection with your child.

Key takeaways from this chapter include:

1. Don't delay: Start your healing journey now.

2. Create a safe, loving, secure environment where your child can express themselves.

3. Foster open and honest communication with your child.

4. Help your child develop emotion-focused and problem-focused coping skills.

5. Work toward being present with your child.

Think about your own coping skills. Where did they come from and how do they work for you?

_____

_____

_____

_____

_____

In an average day, how many hours do you feel you are present? What activities can help you be more present?

_____

_____

_____

Do you feel your child opens up to you and shares their emotions? If not, what steps can you take to encourage communication?

_____

_____

_____

Next Steps

- The next time you are feeling stressed, notice if you utilize problem- or emotion-focused coping skills.

- Become aware of your own mind/body connection by noticing your physical sensations when you feel stressed or anxious or experience any other difficult emotions.

- Find a time during the week when you can be present with your child. Either schedule a "date" outside the home or pick a time to do a fun activity around the house.

CHAPTER FIVE

Managing Your Child's Emotions

This chapter covers how your child might be experiencing your breakup, as well as strategies you can implement to minimize their trauma. Early intervention in getting your co-parenting relationship on track is crucial in order to help your child through this transition smoothly. The process starts with helping your child understand what they are feeling, teaching them how to manage their emotions, and answering their questions the right way so they can have a sense of certainty and security, knowing that you both love them and are willing to make sure their needs will be treated as a priority.

Acknowledge Your Child's Emotions

As stated previously, parents tend to want to protect their children from pain. The fact of the matter is that life is going to involve some painful periods. Your relationship breakup experience, while incredibly painful, gives you an opportunity to create meaning from it by helping your children identify and communicate what they are feeling in a healthy and balanced way. This can have a long-lasting impact on how your child shows up in all their relationships later on in life.

You might be asking, *"How can I acknowledge my child's emotions when they won't share them with me?"* You likely have asked the same questions over and over: "How are you?" "Are you okay?" "What are you feeling?" Perhaps your child just responds with "I'm cool," "I'm okay," or "I'm fine." You know they aren't fine. You can see that your child is more withdrawn. Perhaps they've lost interest in the things they normally like to do. They might be talking back to you more frequently or acting out in other ways, such as getting into fights at school or displaying more aggressive behavior. Perhaps your child's emotions have shown up as slipping grades or poor performance in their extracurricular activities. These are all signs that your child is experiencing stress. To acknowledge your child's emotions, you will need to pay attention to what they are showing you, as well as what they are telling you.

As discussed in chapter 2, your child's executive functioning is not fully developed until they reach adulthood. This is where you come in. You have the very important role of helping your child acknowledge and communicate what they are feeling.

The best way to acknowledge your child's emotions is to simply make yourself emotionally available to them. This means not only creating a safe place for your child to express their feelings, but also helping them identify and name what they are feeling. Using a reflective, empathetic stance, you may need to help your child find the words to express their feelings while normalizing and validating their emotions. Teaching your child how to express what they are feeling will allow them to feel more emotionally regulated and grounded, which, in turn, will improve their behavior and how they function in the world. By showing them how to express what they are feeling, you are not only helping them feel less alone in their experience, but you are also minimizing the trauma they could potentially experience from the transition.

Anger

As mentioned previously, when it comes to understanding the emotions your child is experiencing, pay attention to what they are showing you, as well as what they are telling you. For example, say your normally respectful and well-behaved child is talking back in a disrespectful way. Rather than reacting with your own anger in the moment to the things they said, approach your child when things have settled down. Acknowledge their anger, and then create a space for them to express this anger in a healthier way while maintaining your own emotional regulation. In most cases, you'll find that the anger is acting as a shield to protect the more vulnerable emotion. Once you help them identify and express the more vulnerable emotion, refrain from trying to "fix" it. Simply sit with them as they express the emotion, and reflect and validate what they are experiencing.

After your child has expressed themselves, separate the behavior from the emotion while setting boundaries for the behavior. Gently explain to them that disrespectful language is the behavior and that expressing anger in this way is not acceptable. Then, help them come up with healthier ways of processing their anger.

Confusion

Imagine you are cruising along, living your best life. You love your home and how you have it decorated, you enjoy your job, and you have an active social life. Suddenly, you come home and find out all of that is changing and there is nothing you can do to stop it. You have to move out of the home you love, you're being fired from your job, and you will lose all your friends. Wouldn't you feel confused about why this is happening and have a ton of questions? Maybe you'd feel like the rug was being pulled out from under you. That is likely how your child is feeling right now. When they hear that their parents are splitting up, they immediately will think about all the things they love that could possibly change. They're going to be confused.

It's common to want to protect your child from feeling this confusion by giving them as little information as possible. In some cases, you may be tempted to not tell them anything because, perhaps, you don't know what's going to happen next, either. If you have laid the groundwork outlined in this book up until now, you have everything you need to answer their questions calmly and rationally. When a child doesn't have information, they will fill in the gaps and create a scary story in their head that is probably way worse than the reality of the situation. Later in this chapter, you will read about common questions children ask and how to answer them.

Fear

When a child starts to create a scary story in their head about what is happening because they are feeling confused, they will start to feel afraid. As stated previously, kids like certainty. They like to know what's going to happen. When they don't know what's going to happen, they can get scared. It's up to you to be the calm, rational voice to ease their concerns. It may be tempting to try to cheer them up or minimize what they are feeling to relieve your own anxiety, but it's important to normalize and validate what they are feeling instead. Try to imagine the situation from their perspective. Help them think of a situation that felt scary and out of their control but turned out okay. Sit down with your child and make a list of all the things that will remain the same, so they don't focus so much on what is changing. Stress to your child that you and your co-parent will both do your best to put them at the forefront of every decision going forward. Present a joined and united front where you show them that you can get along and collaborate. Once you move into separate living quarters and start following your custody arrangement, be cordial when you do see each other.

Grief and Loss

A relationship breakup can be a loss similar in magnitude to the death of a family member. According to grief expert Elisabeth Kübler-Ross, the five stages of grief are denial, anger, bargaining, depression, and acceptance. Each child will experience grief in their own unique way. Your child may not experience these stages in this order, and in some cases they may experience more than one stage at a time. In the early stages, your child may present with disbelief, shock, and denial. Later stages of grief may include sadness, anxiety, depression, or acting out in anger. Less obvious signs of grieving may include irritability, hyperactivity, or fear.

The best way to help your child cope with their grief is to talk to them about what they are feeling and validate their emotions. Try to understand your child's grief from their perspective. Normalize their feelings by sharing your own in a way that isn't overwhelming for them. Create a safe environment for them by keeping routine and structure in the home consistent and clearly communicating boundaries. If your child has a hard time verbalizing what they are feeling, create activities where they can express their feelings nonverbally, such as drawing and crafts. Encourage journaling exercises where they can write about their feelings.

Insecurity

Along with fear and confusion comes insecurity. Your normally confident, self-assured child may suddenly become insecure about things that seem random. Maybe they worry excessively about what their peers are thinking or saying about the changes happening in their home life. Younger children may become more clingy or needy with one parent, especially when they are anticipating a change in custody. This can be exacerbated if either of you jumps into the dating pool too soon or attempts to introduce a romantic partner before your child is ready. Focus instead on providing a stable environment in both homes where you are both emotionally and physically available to your child. Structure and routine can go a long way in helping them feel secure. As you focus on smoothing out your co-parenting relationship, your child will begin to feel more secure. When the child is about to change custody, remind them of how much they will enjoy being with the other parent and all the fun things they'll get to do while they are there. If the child is worried about peers, remind them that they can't change what other people are thinking or saying; they only have control over themselves.

Sadness

When a child is feeling sad, it usually presents as tearfulness. Sometimes, the child will seem depressed. It's very important not to tell your child to "stop crying" or try to cheer them up. This will make them feel as though they shouldn't feel this way and that they should feel happier. In turn, they may try to appear happier than they really are to make *you* feel better.

Sadness is a normal part of the human experience, and without it one wouldn't be able to appreciate the joyful times. Tears are a normal human response to sadness, just as laughter is to joy. Encourage your child to cry while reminding them that what they are feeling now won't last forever, and they are in charge of determining how long it will last. If they need to spend some time alone in their room to cry, that's okay.

The Disney/Pixar movie *Inside Out* offers a wonderful explanation of all the human emotions and how they can be integrated. Watch the movie with your child and talk about it afterward. Share your personal experience with sadness, and explain how you were able to overcome your sadness.

Worry

Worry is another word for anxiety. If your child struggles with anxiety, it might initially become worse as a result of the breakup. If your child is normally calm, they may suddenly start to worry. To help your child make sense of what they are feeling, try creating a Worry Wall together. Using sticky notes, have them write down everything they are worried about, one item per sticky note. Once they have all the sticky notes done, help them arrange the sticky notes in order of priority on a wall or door, with the biggest issue they are worried about at the top of the list, working your way down. Act as the child's assistant and let them tell you what they are worried about and direct the order as you place them. As you are doing this, talk to them about each item to get more context around the area of concern by asking open-ended questions. You are just exploring the area of worry with them, not coming up with solutions at this stage. You may be surprised to find out that the relationship breakup isn't the primary area of concern. Your child might be more worried about an upcoming test, game, or recital. Finally, using the problem- and/or emotion-focused coping skills described earlier (page 79), help your child work through some of their worries.

The Importance of Staying Present

There is a common theme among all the emotions your child is feeling. Their thoughts are focused on things that are out of their control, and they aren't feeling present and in the moment. In reality, one only has control over what is happening in the here and now. Mindfulness activities help your child understand why staying present can feel calming. Starting with the emotions outlined in this chapter, help your child understand what is happening in their brain when they are feeling these emotions. This exercise also helps with self-soothing.

1. In a mason jar, mix together a heaping tablespoon of glitter and glue. Then, fill the rest of the jar with water.

2. Put the lid on the jar. Shake it up!

3. Ask your child to pick an emotion that they feel is most pervasive for them in that moment while shaking the jar. As you are shaking the jar, have them talk about the emotion, and reflect back what you are hearing.

4. Set the jar down to see the swirling glitter. Compare this to the thoughts that are swirling around in their head. Normalize this by talking about how hard it is to make decisions or to feel calm when thoughts are swirling in this way.

5. As the glitter starts to settle, demonstrate deep breathing for your child (see page 97). Ask them to do it with you.

6. Once all the glitter has settled, ask your child to describe how they are feeling. Most likely, they will describe a calmer feeling. Encourage them to calm themselves down in this way when they are feeling any negative emotion.

This exercise not only helps children learn about how their emotions can cloud their thoughts, but it also facilitates the practice of mindfulness while focusing on the swirling glitter in the jar.

Mindfulness for Teenagers

How do you get your teenager to give mindfulness a try? Suggest a technology detox. Studies indicate that excessive use of smartphones can lead to mental health issues in teens. Carve out 20 minutes once or twice a week for your teen to put down the smartphone and do a guided meditation. Ideally, it can make the experience even more special if you meditate with them.

A study conducted by researchers from Johns Hopkins indicated that meditation has the same effect on the brain as antidepressants. Encouraging a regular meditation practice for your teen can help them maintain balance in their brain. As they start to see the benefits for themselves, they will be more motivated to keep the practice going!

JOHANA AND JAROD

Johana and Jarod, who recently divorced, have one eight-year-old son together named Ren. They had agreed that Ren would live with Johana and would be in Jarod's custody every other weekend. This arrangement was agreed upon because Jarod, who had a long history of unemployment, had gotten a job and was working a lot of hours trying to obtain some financial security. As they were trying to navigate the early stages of their custody arrangement, Ren alternated between wanting to see his father and saying he missed him during the week when he was with his mother, to not wanting to go to his father's house and acting out when it was time to change custody. Johana, who was the one to initiate the divorce, felt guilty about putting her son through this change, so she would give in and keep Ren in her custody when he would push back about going to his father's. This upset Jarod and caused many escalated arguments between Johana and Jarod.

They eventually sought out the help of a co-parent coach. The coach encouraged them both to stick to the custody schedule, even though Ren was acting out when it was time to go to his father's. The coach also suggested Johana carve out an hour two times a week to go outside and throw the ball with Ren, since that was one of his favorite activities. Over time, as Ren got comfortable with this routine with his mother, Johana started talking to Ren about how he was feeling about the new family dynamic. With patience from Johana, Ren eventually started talking about how much he missed having the family together. He even confessed that he thought if he made it difficult when it was time to go to his father's house, his parents might get back together. Johana maintained an empathetic stance with Ren and did not have a strong reaction when he shared this with her. In their co-parent coaching sessions, Johana, Jarod, and their coach worked together to process the emotions that were coming up for both parents as Ren began opening up. They also worked together to help the co-parents become joined and united in their response to Ren, so they were both empathetic to what he was feeling while maintaining the message that this was the new normal. Eventually, Ren grew accustomed to the new dynamic. He also realized how sharing what he was feeling made him feel better.

Encourage Sharing Emotions

Talking about emotions can have a powerful impact on how your child adjusts post-breakup. Kids who learn to talk about their emotions early on are better able to self-soothe and regulate their stronger emotions later in life. Imagine a pressure cooker: If you attempt to open it before the pressure is released, you have an explosion on your hands. If you release the pressure first, you can open the lid safely. Talking about emotions helps your child release the pressure. Creating a safe place for them to do so helps normalize what they are feeling, which, in turn, decreases anxiety and depression.

You might be wondering how to create a safe place for your child. It starts by becoming comfortable with vulnerability. If your child talks about their emotions and senses that they are making you uncomfortable, they will feel unsafe and stop sharing. Kids are incredibly intuitive, and they will pick up on your discomfort even if you think you aren't showing it. That's why it's so important for you to get comfortable with your own vulnerability. Being able to share your feelings will normalize vulnerability for your child. This doesn't mean comparing what the child is sharing to your life experience or circumstances. For example, let's say your child shares how they are being bullied in school because word has gotten out that their parents are splitting up. Rather than relating to the child by sharing an example of when you were bullied (which can feel like you are making the conversation be about yourself, from the child's perspective), put yourself in your child's shoes while imagining what that must feel like for them. Perhaps you understand because you once felt that way. Understanding what your child is experiencing using feeling words is how you express empathy.

In some cases, a parent may become reactive when their child shares something they don't want to hear. Parents can create a safe space by being receptive and welcoming, versus reactive, when their child appears to be upset. As your child grows, they will develop opinions that may not align with yours. To create a safe place for them, it's important to accept that this is how they become their own person separate from you. Expressing their opinions and knowing you might not agree can feel scary. Once you've ensured that the child feels safe to express themselves, you can encourage activities to help them self-soothe.

Helping Your Child Make the Mind and Body Connection

Start helping your child understand what they are feeling in their body by guiding them through a body scan when they are feeling upset.

1. Sitting comfortably in a chair, have your child close their eyes and do a body scan, slowly scanning their body, starting at the top of the head and moving down to their toes.

2. Have your child describe what sensations they are feeling and where the sensations are in their body.

3. Using the following table, ask them to rank on a scale of 1 to 10 how strong the sensation is in that particular area of the body. This helps build their mind/body awareness.

Once they have this awareness, help your child implement a mindfulness activity, such as deep breathing, to self-soothe.

1. Slowly inhale, imagining that you are breathing in a healing light while counting to 4. Hold the breath for half a second.

2. Then, slowly exhale, imagining that you are breathing out a toxic fume (to represent all the negative emotions) while counting to 4. Hold the exhale for half a second.

3. Do this three to five times.

Parents can help the child check back in with their body by doing another body scan after the activity, again ranking sensations from 1 to 10, to see if they notice an improvement in how their body feels.

DATE/TIME	SENSATION (WHAT/ WHERE IN THE BODY)	RANK 1–10	DEEP BREATHING EXERCISE	RANK 1–10

Emotional Charades

Helping your child build emotional intelligence will increase their ability to identify and communicate what they are feeling. They will also develop higher emotional intelligence later in life. You can make this fun by turning it into a game. The cards can also be used when your child is feeling an emotion that they are having a hard time articulating. You can give them the cards and ask them to pick the one that best describes how they are feeling.

1. List out several positive and negative emotions on index cards, one emotion per card. Include an emoji or picture to illustrate the emotion.

2. Shuffle the cards and take turns with your child pulling from the stack of cards.

3. Act out the emotion without using words until the other person correctly guesses the emotion.

Following is a list of example emotions that you can write on the cards. Feel free to add any emotions not listed here:

Happy	🙂
Sad	🙁
Angry	😠
Worried	😟
Annoyed	😖
Excited	😃
Irritated	😒

Answering Your Child's Questions

Telling your child that you are breaking up can feel like a daunting task. Usually, there is a lot of angst around how the conversation will go and how to answer questions they might ask. Generally speaking, the first conversation is usually a short one. There may be some tears, but your child may be too overwhelmed to ask questions right away. In some cases, especially for younger children, they might not quite "get it" until one of the parents moves out and the custody exchange begins. No matter the age of your child, it's best to anticipate and plan for questions that may come at the time of the initial conversation or later, once they have had time to process.

This section covers common questions that your child may ask you and examples of better and worse ways to answer them. As your child asks questions, try to pick up on the distress underneath the question and reflect that back in an empathetic way. It's important to take time to consider the question and make sure you understand exactly what they are asking, verbally and emotionally, before you answer. You may not have answers for all of their questions, and that's okay. You can take some time to consider your response if you need to do so. Just make sure you tell them you want to give them a thoughtful response and need some time to think about it, then honor your promise to come back to it later with an answer. It's crucial that you don't point fingers, place blame, or talk negatively about each other as you answer your child's questions.

Why is this happening?

This is one of the most common questions you'll hear from your child. It's common to feel you are protecting them by not answering it or by not giving them any explanation. This will cause them to create their own story about what is happening and blame themselves. It's important to help your child understand that your love for them is unconditional and will never change, even though your feelings for each other have changed. You also want to reassure them that you both are committed to minimizing the impact of this change on their life.

Example of a Correct Response: *"Your Dad and I realized that we don't get along well anymore. Our feelings for each other have changed. We've decided that we would get along better and fight less if we live apart. We both love* you, and that will never change. We want to make this as easy on you as possible and will work together to make sure you're taken care of."

Example of an Incorrect Response: *"Your Dad had an affair with his secretary and he's the reason why we are breaking up. You can blame him."*

Why don't you love each other anymore?

Your child is likely asking this question because their love for you is unconditional, and they don't understand how feelings can change. It's important to take some responsibility here and present this in a neutral way, even though it might be tempting to point fingers if one of you is still in love with the other person.

Example of a Correct Response: *"Over the course of our relationship, we allowed certain things to take priority over our relationship, and, as a result, we grew apart. We started arguing so much that our feelings for each other changed."* This next part is appropriate if you have an amicable breakup: *"We still care about each other as co-parents to you, but our love for each other has changed."*

Example of an Incorrect Response: *"I still love your mom but she apparently doesn't love me anymore since she chose this."*

Do you still love me?

Again, your child is asking this question because they are worried that if your feelings have changed for each other, your feelings could possibly change for them, too. It's important to emphasize this point more than once to make sure they are aware that your love for them is different and unchangeable. It's also important to form a joined and united front as you share this message and assure them that they are a priority, and you will still work together to make sure their needs are met. Having said this, don't make promises that you can't deliver on. Set realistic expectations.

Example of a Correct Response: *"We both love you unconditionally, and that will never change. We will always be your parents and will make your needs our priority with every decision we make. We can't guarantee that we* will never disagree, but we will always work toward being cordial with each other out of our love for you."

Example of an Incorrect Response: *"Apparently, your dad doesn't love you as much as I do since he is the one who wants to leave and break up our family."*

Is this my fault?

Kids will always find a way to blame themselves, and they won't always share with you the story they have created in their heads about how the breakup is their fault. It's important to anticipate that and address it right up front, even if they don't ask you this question.

Example of a Correct Response: *"We are to blame for our relationship breaking up. Sometimes people grow apart, and their feelings change for each other. Although we worked to fix it, we determined it wasn't fixable. This has nothing to do with you, and there isn't anything you did to cause this."*

Example of an Incorrect Response: *"Well, if I hadn't had to work two jobs to pay for all your sports maybe I would have been home more, and she wouldn't be leaving me."*

When will you live with each other again?

Kids don't like change. When they hear about the breakup for the first time, their grief starts immediately. This question is a combination of resisting change and the denial phase of grief. They don't want to face the fact that change is happening and that both parents, whom they love, won't be living under the same roof anymore. It's important to give them language that is aligned with the "new normal" and keep that language consistent across both parents to present as a united front.

Example of a Correct Response: *"I can understand that you are struggling with this change. When I have felt this way, I just wanted things to go back to the way they used to be so I would feel less scared and anxious about the unknown future. Unfortunately, we won't be living together again, but we will still love you from two different households. We will still be a family; it's just taking on a new form. It will take some time to get to a new normal as a family, but we'll get there together."*

Example of an Incorrect Response: *"If he breaks up with his girlfriend maybe he'll be back."*

Emotional Uno

This exercise is a unique spin on a game kids already love to play: Uno. The basic rules of Uno still apply. The goal of Uno is for a player to get rid of their cards. When a player only has one card remaining, they yell out "Uno!"

You may choose to have each color represent an emotion, or only give an example of an emotion when a card in a certain color is drawn. If you choose to have each card indicate an emotion, some examples are as follows:

Red cards: Angry   Yellow cards: Happy   Wild: Scared/anxious

Green cards: Grateful   Blue cards: Sad

1. Each player is dealt seven cards facedown.

2. The remaining cards are placed facedown in a pile with one card flipped over beside it to start the discard pile.

3. Each player must follow what the top card in the discard pile indicates by either number, color, or action.

4. If the player has a card that they can play, then they will discard it when it is their turn. When the player discards a card, they will give an example of when they felt the emotion that corresponds to the color of the discarded card.

5. If the player does not have a card that they can play, then they must draw a new card from the draw pile.

6. When a player has only one card left in their hand, they must yell "Uno!" If they don't, and another player catches them, they must pick up two cards.

7. The first player to discard all their cards wins!

Chapter Takeaways

Here are some key takeaways from this chapter to help your child gently move through this transition. Don't forget to include lots of hugs!

1. Gain a clear understanding of what specific emotions your child might be feeling.

2. Help them put words to what they are feeling while normalizing and validating them.

3. Provide them with techniques to develop mind/body awareness.

4. Teach them exercises to help with mindfulness and self-soothing.

5. Answer your child's questions honestly while avoiding pointing fingers at each other.

As you read through this chapter, what are some parenting tips that are new for you that you will start to incorporate?

_____

_____

_____

_____

Now that you have a better understanding of the common emotions your child might be experiencing, what emotions do you feel are specific to your child?

_____

_____

_____

_____

Reflecting on the list of sample questions your child might ask, how might you reframe some of your answers to fit your specific situation?

_____

_____

_____

_____

Next Steps

Doing the work outlined in this chapter can be challenging. Most people will agree they want their kids to be okay during a parental break-up. Early intervention is crucial to getting a co-parenting relationship in place the right way. Here are the next steps to build on the knowledge you gained in this chapter:

- Listen to a co-parenting podcast to keep your mindset in the right place.

- Notice if your child might be reflecting back to you what you are feeling. Is there a connection?

- Develop your own mindfulness by doing some of the exercises in this chapter before trying them with your child.

- With your co-parent, talk through some of the questions you feel your child might ask, and come up with a script on how to answer them so you're both on the same page.

CHAPTER SIX

Healing Yourself

n order for you each to be the best parent you can be to your child, you both need to operate as your best selves. How do you do that when you are dealing with your own grief from the breakup? Or perhaps you're not grieving, but instead you're feeling overwhelmed by the anxiety of an unknown future. Whether or not you chose the breakup can sometimes determine your emotional experience. If you chose the breakup, perhaps you moved through much of your grief as you were making the determination that the relationship wasn't fixable. If you didn't choose the breakup and you still had hope things would work out, you may just be starting to grieve now. The intention is that as you read this chapter, you will feel validated about what you are feeling and will walk away with the tools you need to heal yourself and manage your emotions in a healthy way.

Healing yourself starts with acknowledging and taking responsibility for what you are feeling so you can become empowered to manage your emotional experience. As you are learning how to do this, you are experiencing personal growth that will last the rest of your life. You will also have the tools to help your children manage their emotions in a healthy way. As you heal yourself, you can help your child heal. You will notice that as you get better, they get better, too.

Acknowledge Your Own Emotions

The end of a relationship and not knowing what the future holds combined with worry about your child's well-being can cause a roller coaster of emotions for you as a parent. The more you acknowledge your own emotions as you move through this transition, the better you will be at helping your child through it, too. You will be modeling healthy vulnerability and coping mechanisms for your child.

Learning how to embrace your feelings and express vulnerability will strengthen your emotional connections in all of your relationships. Feeling unexpressed pain can result in creating stories in your head about situations and then reacting based on these stories, which may or may not be accurate. When you are dealing with the emotions associated with grieving a breakup, this tendency can be heightened. Being honest about what is factual and what is an emotionally driven story you've created before you respond can have a big impact on how appropriate your reaction is.

Give yourself some grace. Everyone experiences emotional pain, and most people are unaware of the impact it has on their relationships. Vulnerability is often considered a weakness, but being honest about what you are feeling and being willing to face your more difficult emotions is actually a strength!

Whether or not you chose the breakup, it's important to recognize that there is a grieving process happening. Start by being honest with yourself about what you are feeling, and try not to suppress those feelings. The only way out of the grieving process is through it. What you resist will persist, and in the process you will deny yourself your grieving process. Denying your grief, distracting yourself from it, or using unhealthy coping mechanisms will only prolong the grief. Even if you are happy or relieved about the breakup, there is likely some fear and anxiety about the future that you need to address.

Following are some common emotions that are associated with the grieving process, along with some strategies for how to manage these emotions in a constructive way.

Anger

If you didn't choose the breakup, you may be feeling angry at the other person for initiating it. Perhaps your partner didn't handle the breakup well, and you are feeling as though you no longer matter to them. It's important to recognize that anger is a secondary emotion acting as a protective shield for the "soft underbelly" of a more vulnerable emotion, such as feeling hurt, abandoned, rejected, or betrayed. Processing the anger as a way of getting to the more vulnerable emotion can be very effective. Can you recall a time when you started out yelling at someone and ended up crying? That's because you got the anger out and were able to access the more vulnerable emotion. Processing the anger in a productive way in order to excavate the more vulnerable emotion can be incredibly powerful. It's important to not shame yourself for feeling the anger.

- You can process the anger by going to an isolated area where no one can hear you and screaming at the top of your lungs, or you can scream into a pillow if leaving the home isn't an option.

- Write a letter to your ex, letting the swear words fly, but don't send it. Burn it or tear it up instead. Before destroying it, rewrite the letter as many times as you need to until you feel you have gotten all your anger out.

- Put a picture of your ex on an empty chair and yell at it. Write down what you are feeling in your journal.

Bitterness

Sometimes when you hold on to anger for too long, internalizing it, that anger can turn into bitterness. With bitterness, there is an element of sadness. Perhaps you are obsessed with how you were treated unfairly in the relationship or how poorly your ex handled the breakup. This tends to happen when you focus on what was done to you rather than redirecting that energy toward accepting your contribution to the demise of that relationship. When someone is bitter for a long time, they can paint any potential romantic partner with a broad sweeping brush, projecting their bitterness onto them. For example, you might hear yourself saying things like "all men are jerks" or "all women are crazy." This is a sign that you may be overemphasizing your role as a victim and could miss the opportunity to learn about yourself from the relationship. Shifting your mindset away from what was done to you and toward what you can learn about yourself can be incredibly empowering. Holding on to anger is like throwing gas on ourselves and expecting the other person to burn.

List out all the situations where you feel you were treated poorly. Then, list what you learned about yourself that you will carry forward to improve how you show up in your relationships.

Fear

The Oxford Languages dictionary defines fear as "a feeling of anxiety concerning the outcome of something or the safety and well-being of someone." Fear is a very common emotion, whether you chose the breakup or not. Sometimes the fear is about the scary unknown future, and perhaps someone is fearful for their physical safety if they are leaving an abusive relationship. When human beings experience change and don't know what's coming next, fear will often bubble up. This emotion is often underneath some of the other emotions referenced in this chapter.

If you are leaving an abusive relationship, it is crucial that you have a safety plan in place to protect yourself and your children. A therapist can help you develop one, or you can create your own from the National Domestic Violence Hotline website (see References for the link, page 135).

No matter where your fear is coming from, when you are feeling fearful, you typically aren't operating from the more logical part of the brain. It's common to obsessively focus on areas outside of your control, creating worst-case scenarios, making negative predictions about the future, or "othering," which is focusing on someone else's thoughts, feelings, behaviors, or actions. This can feel very disempowering, so it is important to redirect your thoughts to areas that are within your locus of control. You will find an exercise to help with this at the end of this chapter.

Sadness

Sadness seems to be more pervasive in the early stages of the grieving process, although it can pop up randomly further down the road. Tearfulness is an obvious sign of feeling sad, but sadness can also show up as feeling mildly depressed in general. If you chose the breakup, you may have experienced more sadness as you were coming to terms with the fact that you needed to end the relationship. If you didn't choose it, you're likely experiencing sadness after the breakup has occurred. A common way of distracting oneself from feeling sad is by staying busy or by self-medicating with drugs, food, alcohol, or other compulsive behaviors. It's common to jump into the dating pool too soon when you feel sad, which can make you feel worse in the long run.

If you can lean into the sadness, it will eventually pass. The sadness one feels in divorce or separation is like sitting in the dark earth with the roots that will eventually grow into something beautiful. Imagine that your tears are watering that earth. Methods to process your sadness include journaling your feelings and proactively carving out time to allow yourself to cry.

Guilt

Guilt is common when you are the one who chose the breakup, but this emotion can also be experienced by someone who feels regret around their actions or behaviors that led up to the breakup. Often, a person will feel guilty when they caused another person emotional pain, such as choosing to break up with them, and are "owning" that person's feelings. Guilt can also stem from regret over things that happened in the past that can't be changed.

It's important to realize that owning someone else's feelings is not going to make those feelings go away. If you handled the breakup poorly, making amends in the form of a letter, email, or face-to-face conversation is helpful to provide closure for the other party, but let them be responsible for their feelings while you focus on your own. The same applies to guilt associated with regrets about your role in the demise of the relationship. Making a sincere, heartfelt apology can help with healing and is the right thing to do, and in doing so, you are showing the other party grace and compassion, but it won't make the other party's feelings go away.

Hurt

Hurt can show up in the context of a relationship breakup as feeling abandoned, betrayed, or rejected by the other party. Perhaps you chose the breakup and feel let down that your expectations for the relationship were not realized. It can feel as though you are literally wounded emotionally. Hurt can often show up as anger, which can feel like a "safer" emotion. Sitting with your hurt can feel very vulnerable. As with the other negative emotions referenced in this section, it's important to sit with those feelings of hurt and try to make sense of exactly what you are going through in order for it to pass. Journaling about the root of the pain can help you make sense of what you are feeling. It is helpful to identify where you are feeling the pain in your physical body. Once you pinpoint where you are feeling it, breathe beautiful light representing healing and love into that area of your body, and breathe out the toxic pain.

Resentment

Like bitterness, resentment often shows up when you've been angry for an extended period of time. Perhaps you started out feeling angry about certain things that the other party did in the relationship, but you swept your feelings under the rug rather than dealing with them in a healthy way. Over time, as those issues accumulate, you will feel resentful toward the other person. This is a common emotion when someone feels that they have given more than the other person in the relationship. It is also common for someone who has codependent relationship patterns to feel resentment.

It is important to use your breakup to learn about yourself and examine why you are feeling resentment. Resentment and bitterness can spill over into your other relationships, such as those with friends, family, and co-workers, causing them damage as well. As stated previously, as you move forward into a new relationship, it's common to project resentment and bitterness onto the new romantic partner unfairly, thus making them pay for crimes they didn't commit. Redirect that energy toward yourself, and focus on what you can learn about your role in the demise of the relationship instead of focusing so much on what was done to you.

Relief

Not all emotions following a breakup are negative. Sometimes, making the decision to leave a toxic, unhealthy situation can feel empowering. If there was a lot of conflict in your relationship, or if there was a general sense of pain, resentment, or bitterness, you might feel relieved when you realize you are now living in a peaceful environment. It's common for relief to be tied up with guilt, because you are aware that you caused the other person pain by choosing to end the relationship. It's important to be aware that if the person you were with was bringing out your worst qualities, it was probably for the best to end the relationship, even if you both feel some pain from the breakup. Now you are both free to find someone who brings out your best.

As you can see, there is some overlap with these emotions. There may be some negative emotions that you don't see represented here, such as abandonment or betrayal. You might feel very alone in your pain, as if no one quite understands what you are going through. What you are feeling is a normal part of any loss. Just be assured that there will be an end to your grieving process if you honor it and use it as an opportunity to grow and learn about yourself. Personal growth isn't always pleasant. Sometimes it hurts. You will reap the rewards later by not only being less anxious and depressed, but also being more present with more peace and tranquility in your life.

Visualizing to Heal Negative Emotions

Use this visualization exercise when you are feeling hurt, angry, resentful, or bitter toward your ex. It may be difficult at first, but with persistence, it not only helps you heal these emotions, but it can also have a powerful impact on how you show up with each other as co-parents.

1. Sit in a comfortable chair in a quiet room.

2. Take three deep breaths while visually scanning your body from the top of your head to the tips of your toes, relaxing each area.

3. When you are feeling completely relaxed, imagine your former partner doing something that they love. If you can't think of something that they love to do, just imagine that they are happy.

4. Imagine them surrounded by beautiful green healing light, smiling joyfully. Imagine the green light slowly turning to white, representing the cleansing of the past.

5. If you notice any resentment surfacing as you do this exercise, just observe it. Over time, the resentment should start to dissipate, and you will be able to be more cordial with your co-parent.

Incorporating Deep Breathing into Your Day

You have probably noticed that deep breathing is recommended frequently throughout this book. Deep breathing has been proven to stimulate your vagus nerve, which runs along your spine and connects your brain with the important organs in your body. By activating the vagus nerve, you are increasing the response of the parasympathetic nervous system, thus increasing relaxation. You can activate it with slow, abdominal breathing. When many people attempt deep breathing, they suck in their gut and fill up their chest. Let's look at the correct way to deep breathe.

1. Intentionally fill up your belly as you take a slow, deep breath.

2. As you are breathing in, notice how the breath feels as it flows through your mouth, down your trachea, through your lungs, and into your belly.

3. Observe any sensations you might feel without judgment. Just notice them.

4. Over time, you may start to notice some tingling in your head or throughout your body, or you may find a general feeling of calmness.

Deep breathing can be incorporated throughout your day. Take a 5-minute deep breathing break during the workday or while the kids are taking a nap. You can even do it while sitting at a stoplight or while lying in bed.

IVAN AND DALE

Ivan, a single dad of a 13-year-old son named Dale, was devastated when his boyfriend broke up with him. Although the relationship had been unhealthy for a number of years and their sex life had dried up, Ivan had always hoped the relationship would improve. When his partner left him for another person, Ivan felt betrayed, rejected, and abandoned. As he started to make sense of his feelings, he began to realize that both he and his boyfriend drank heavily on the weekends and that most of their fights happened when they had been drinking. Dale, who experienced anxiety, had pointed this out to Ivan over the years, but Ivan had ignored him. When Ivan got honest with himself, he realized his drinking had been an issue in many of his relationships, since he tended to become aggressive when he drank.

Ivan made the decision to give up alcohol. He realized he was going to need some help, so he started working with a therapist who specialized in substance use disorder and found a Buddhist center where he could develop a meditation practice. Ivan also decided to clean up his nutrition, and he became a vegetarian. Dale, who was excited to see his dad make these positive changes, started meditating with him. As Ivan started meditating, he started to notice that his anxiety around letting go of his negative coping mechanisms was starting to ease. He noticed that he was becoming calmer and more present. Dale, in turn, also started to relax and enjoy himself more. Normally a quiet, withdrawn teenager, he started to develop more friendships, and he was smiling and laughing more often. As Ivan became more convinced that these changes were serving his highest and best good, his resolve strengthened. He informed all of his friends of his new lifestyle and let go of those friends who weren't supportive of these positive changes. Now, Ivan has been sober and a vegetarian for two years and is involved in a healthy relationship with someone he met at the Buddhist center who supports the new, evolved version of himself. Dale, who now feels heard and validated regularly, is thriving.

Understanding Your Emotional Triggers

Anytime you feel a strong emotional reaction to something, there is usually a trigger, or something that pushed a button inside of you to cause the reaction. Understanding your triggers can help you manage your emotional reactions. In order for you both to transition into a healthy co-parenting relationship, it's important to understand and take accountability for your emotional triggers, including what they are, how you responded to them while you were still together, and how you will respond to them now as co-parents. If you are honest with yourselves, you each may see some repeating patterns from previous relationships.

It can be difficult to identify and own our triggers, because it is common to blame the other person for our emotional reaction and point to something they did to us. While you may be justified in being upset about what the other person did, the trigger and the resulting emotional state are completely your own.

Oftentimes, triggers stem from events that happened in childhood or trauma that we experienced during our life. It is important to treat yourself with grace and compassion as you explore the root of your triggers. Understanding where your triggers come from is the first step toward empowering yourself to manage your emotional reactions. If you both can own your triggers and your emotional reactions, you can completely transform your co-parenting relationship.

ABCs of Understanding Cognitive Distortions

Let's practice understanding cognitive distortions. In this exercise, you will fill out the ABCs of cognitive distortions.

A stands for **Activating Event** and is where you will identify what is triggering your strong emotional reaction. For example: *"My co-parent isn't responding to my texts."*

B stands for **Underlying Belief**, or the thought that is driving the emotional response. For example: *"My co-parent is ghosting me/trying to manipulate me/living their best life, and I don't matter to them."*

C stands for **Consequence**, or how the emotional reaction shows up for you physically. For example: becoming tearful, poor focus, poor sleep, increased or decreased appetite, anger, headache, nausea, shakiness, rapid heartbeat, and/or tension throughout the body.

Fill out the table below, writing one trigger in column A and five examples in columns B and C.

A	B	C
_____	1. _____ 2. _____ 3. _____ 4. _____ 5. _____	1. _____ 2. _____ 3. _____ 4. _____ 5. _____

Redirecting Cognitive Distortions

As a result of what you have learned so far, can you see the connection between the mind and body? The thoughts are the "motor" that drives the physical sensations, and that's where you have some control. Those thoughts are referred to as *cognitive distortions*, and they usually fall in one of these categories (think PROSE):

1. **Predictions**, often negative, about an unknown future

2. **Regrets** around the past that you can't change

3. **Othering**, or focusing on another's thoughts, feelings, actions, and decisions

4. **Story-making** when you don't know the facts

5. **Extreme thinking**, or worst-case scenario thinking, also known as *catastrophizing*

There is a common theme to these PROSE categories: "outside of your control."

When you begin to feel cognitive distortions occurring, step away and do something that feels calming: deep breathing, taking a walk, listening to calming music, doing yoga, napping. You may need a day or two to get back to a relaxed state, depending on how triggered you feel. Once your nervous system has settled and you feel calm, reassess the thoughts, asking yourself the following questions:

- *What is within my control?*

- *What thoughts are based in fact as I know it right now?*

- *Is there evidence against what I am thinking?*

- *What would a trusted friend or family member say about this thought?*

- *What action can I take right now to improve this situation?*

- *What choice honors the highest and best version of myself?*

> ### POSITIVITY PAUSE
>
> *We empower ourselves to acknowledge and take responsibility for our triggers and our emotional reactions when we feel triggered. We commit to making this change so we can be the best co-parents for our child while modeling healthy communication skills.*

Seek Support

If you are trying some of the exercises in this chapter and feeling stuck, enlisting the help of a qualified therapist can help. Assuming you get the assistance you need early on and are able to utilize some of the strategies outlined in this book, your stronger emotions will subside over time. Having said this, when you're dealing with grief and feeling emotional while at the same time needing to co-parent with the person who caused you pain, it's helpful to have a team of support around you. Let's take a few moments to look at resources that are available to help you through this transition.

Co-Parenting Counseling or Coaching

There is an important distinction to make between co-parent counseling/coaching and couple's counseling. There is a common misconception that co-parent counseling/coaching will focus on issues from the past. While this may occur in couple's counseling where the goal is to repair the relationship, that is not the goal in co-parent counseling/coaching. These sessions tend to be more child-centered and focused on tools for conflict resolution, establishing boundaries, and methods to improve communication. No time is dedicated to process past issues, including the circumstances of the breakup and each person's feelings around those issues. These sessions are focused on the *here* and *now* and how to move forward to form a new relationship dynamic that is focused on the kid(s). A co-parent counselor/coach is trained to be neutral and will not take sides as they work with the co-parents to improve their relationship.

Parent Coordinator

A parent coordinator is not a therapist or coach but a neutral third party with specialized training who is looking out for the best interests of the child. In some states in the United States, a parent coordinator can be court ordered when co-parents can't get along; in other states, a recommendation for a parent coordinator can be made in the separation agreement. Co-parents can also voluntarily retain the services of a parent coordinator after they are through the legal process.

A parent coordinator can make recommendations on the custody agreement and can help with dispute resolution. They are also copied on any correspondence that occurs between the co-parents and offer guidance on how to improve communication. If the parent coordinator is court ordered, in some cases they will make the final written recommendation if the co-parents cannot reach an agreement on a certain topic.

If your relationship with your co-parent is high-conflict, working with a parent coordinator can make a big difference in your experience with your co-parent. The parent coordinator can also keep you out of court, thus relieving stress for all parties involved.

Co-Parent Mediator

A co-parent mediator is a neutral third party who can sit down with both of you and help you with your parenting agreement. This is a great resource if you both feel stuck in reaching an agreement on your own. They do not side with either party and are there to give guidance on certain areas where the co-parents are unsure on what choice is best for the child. You can also utilize a co-parent mediator to renegotiate your parenting agreement after trying it out and finding that certain plans you had agreed upon are no longer working.

Friends and Family

When going through this transition and dealing with the grieving process, which can produce overwhelming emotions, it's tempting to lean heavily on friends and family for support. You may find yourself oversharing with anyone who will listen. It's important to think through your boundaries and which friends/family members you trust enough to share your emotional experience. You are vulnerable right now and need to make sure you share your vulnerability with people who are going to provide a safe place for you. Think about your closest relationships as they relate to accessing rooms in your home. There are people you will allow in the bathroom with you, and then there are people who can come into the bedroom but not the bathroom. Maybe there are other people you will let into the kitchen but not upstairs. Finally, there are people who can come into the yard but not into the house. This applies to your friends *and* family. As you think through this analogy, you will likely realize that you've been oversharing with yard people. Be careful about who you share with, and stay mindful of whether you are overburdening the people you do trust. If you feel you are overburdening them, it's time to consider other sources of support, such as an individual therapist with skills and training to help you process your grief or a local or online community dedicated to working through the issues you're processing.

DEALING WITH UNSUPPORTIVE FRIENDS AND FAMILY

As you think through the closest people to you in your life and how you want to establish boundaries, consider who has your child's best interests at heart and who may have their own agenda or be projecting their own issues onto your situation. Those friends and family may not be supportive of the new co-parenting relationship you are trying to establish. Maybe they have negative feelings about what went on in the previous relationship or how you were treated. Perhaps they have only heard one side of the story and are giving you advice that is biased. Or, maybe they are giving you bad advice, even though their intentions are good. It's important that you establish clear boundaries and lines of communication with these people as you work toward establishing the new co-parenting relationship. If you feel they don't have your or your child's best interests at heart, you may need to limit what you share with them.

Support Groups

As you are trying to navigate this new co-parenting dynamic while dealing with triggers and grief, a support group can be a wonderful option to help you through the transition. Co-parenting can feel isolating, and being surrounded by others who are feeling the same way can be nurturing and supportive. There is a unique healing energy that happens in a group of people who are sharing the same experience that is hard to describe. A support group can also be a great alternative if you can't afford individual therapy.

It is best to seek out groups that are run by someone with specialized training, preferably a therapist or co-parent counselor/coach. A well-trained leader will make sure certain boundaries are established and that the group feels safe for all participants. A good group will also have a psychoeducational component where you will learn skills on how to improve your co-parenting relationship. See the Resources section (page 132) to learn how to find groups in your area. If you can't find an in-person group, an online support group is the next best thing.

Online Communities

Online communities are becoming more common. They allow you to connect with others who share your experience from the comfort of your own home. Some online resources take the form of classes, while others are in the form of a support group with some psychoeducation included. Finally, some resources are available through groups on social media that allow people to connect and create community. See the Resources section (page 132) for some of the more well-known online options.

Make Self-Care a Priority

Commit to prioritizing your self-care. Use the following 7-day calendar as a guide, or block out time on your phone's calendar to hold yourself accountable for a daily self-care routine. Journal about where you are now, and then do this again 30 days from now to see if there is an improvement.

SUNDAY	Take a walk in nature
MONDAY	5-minute deep breathing break at 10:00 and at 3:00
TUESDAY	Take a yoga class
WEDNESDAY	5-minute deep breathing break at 10:00 and at 3:00
THURSDAY	Meditation day! 20-minute guided meditation
FRIDAY	Listen to a podcast on improving mental health
SATURDAY	Plan an activity and practice being present with your kid(s)

Create a Vision Board

Sometimes when you are in a dark place, it's difficult to see a way out. This is a great time to create a vision board. Vision boards help you tune in to the feeling state associated with positive change. This exercise can also help you visualize what that positive change might look like.

1. Assemble a bunch of magazines, some scissors, glue, and thick foam poster board.

2. Start cutting out pictures and words that align with the highest and best version of yourself and glue them to the board.

3. Include pictures of your ideal future, even if you aren't quite sure how you will make it happen.

4. As you are doing this exercise, notice any limiting beliefs that are bubbling up.

5. Tune in to what you are feeling in your body. Are you feeling inspired? Hopeful? Excited? Then you are on the right track!

6. Once complete, display the vision board in a place where you can reflect on it periodically.

Chapter Takeaways

Acknowledging and taking responsibility for your emotions is the first step in healing. As you heal, your child will heal. Learning healthier coping strategies will give you the tools you need to help your child cope. Figuring out your triggers and the mind/body response to these triggers helps you manage your emotions in a healthier way. Following are five key lessons from this chapter:

1. Identify and acknowledge your emotions.

2. Develop a routine of self-care and make it a priority.

3. Manage your cognitive distortions, and reach out for help if you need to.

4. Develop a team of support.

5. Establish appropriate boundaries with friends and family members.

Who are the friends and family members you trust and can rely on when you need emotional support?

_____

_____

_____

What are some of the coping strategies mentioned in this chapter that you can commit to putting into practice?

_____

_____

_____

What insight did you gain about yourself from this chapter?

_____

_____

_____

Next Steps

As each parent embarks on their own healing journey, the personal growth begins. The grief that comes from any loss can feel overwhelming, but on the other side of it is an opportunity to become a better version of yourself with not only a stronger co-parenting relationship, but also better relationships with everyone in your life. Believe it or not, it is possible to get along better as co-parents than you did when you were a couple.

- As you interact with people throughout this week, notice when you feel triggered and what that feels like in your body. Write it down in your journal or make a note in your phone.

- Ask a trusted friend to remind you of some of your positive qualities that you may have forgotten about in your grief. Compare yourself now to that version of yourself, and write down some actions you can take to get back there.

- Most people are unaware of their thinking and how it can impact their mood. Start paying attention to your mindset and how it influences your mood.

Resources

Co-Parenting Apps

Co-parenting apps are great tools to streamline communication and documentation when parenting from two households. Following are some well-known apps.

- Our Family Wizard: OurFamilyWizard.com

- Coparently: Coparently.com

- 2houses: 2houses.com

- Peaceful CoParenting: PeacefulParentApp.com

Co-Parent Coaches

Co-parent coaches can be invaluable in helping co-parents establish their new co-parenting relationship. Google co-parent coaches in your area, or check out the following national associations:

- National Association of Divorce Professionals: TheNADP.com

- Conscious Co-Parenting Institute: ConsciousCoparentingInstitute.com

Co-Parenting Class

Bill Eddy is a world-renowned expert on co-parenting in high-conflict situations. He offers a co-parenting class for everyone, regardless of whether their relationship is high-conflict. You can find it here: OnlineParentingPrograms.com/online-classes/bill-eddy.html

Family Mediators

Family mediators are great resources to help with your parenting plan. Check out the following associations to find a mediator in your area.

- Academy of Professional Family Mediators: APFMnet.org
- National Association of Certified Mediators (NACM): MediatorCertification.org
- Association for Conflict Resolution: ACRnet.org
- International Academy of Collaborative Professionals: CollaborativePractice.com

In-Person Support Groups

Try searching Google or Meetup.com to find an in-person group in your area. You can also try PsychologyToday.com, where you can search for groups by zip code.

Online Support Groups

Online support groups are great for connecting with others from the comfort of your own home. Note that online support groups can change over time. Here are the most current resources as of the writing of this book:

- Co-Parenting Support Group: Facebook.com/groups /CoparentingSupportGroup
- Coparenting & Blended Family Support Group: Facebook.com /groups/2608836152469891
- Co-parenting Moms: Sharing the Struggle: Facebook.com /groups/801463370308079
- The Co-Parent Coach: CoparentCoach.biz

Resources for Children

- Rainbows for All Children: Rainbows.org/services/divorce-support

- *Inside Out*, a Disney/Pixar film. This is a wonderful movie to watch with your child to normalize emotions and learn how they can become integrated.

- The Ungame by TaliCor. Play this game with your child to help build emotional intelligence.

- Cover a poster board with pictures of your children making faces that represent various emotions. You can show them faces of other children expressing emotions as examples. Later, when they are upset and having a hard time expressing themselves, have them point to the picture that best represents how they feel. Here is a resource to help: Challenging Behavior.cbcs.usf.edu/docs/FeelingFaces_chart_template.pdf.

- *Mindfulness for Kids: 50 Mindfulness Activities for Kindness, Focus and Calm* by Whitney Stewart and Mina Braun. This card game is great for anyone ages 4 to 104 to help build mindfulness.

References

Ackerman, Courtney E. "25 Fun Mindfulness Activities for Children and Teens." PositivePsychology.com. January 9, 2020. PositivePsychology.com /mindfulness-for-children-kids-activities.

Alavi, Seyyed Salman, Maryam Ghanizadeh, Malihe Farahani, Fereshteh Jannat-ifard, Sudeh Esmaili Alamuti, and Mohammad Reza Mohammadi. "Addictive Use of Smartphones and Mental Disorders in University Students." *Iranian Journal of Psychiatry* 15, no. 2 (April 2020): 96–104. NCBI.NLM.NIH.gov/pmc /articles/PMC7215249.

Alvernia University. "4 Types of Communication Styles." March 27, 2018. Accessed August 2, 2021. online.Alvernia.edu/articles/4-types-co mmunication-styles.

Booth Church, Ellen, Carla Poole, and Susan A. Miller. "Ages & Stages: All About Me." Scholastic EarlyChildhoodToday. Accessed August 2, 2021. Scholastic.com/teachers/articles/teaching-content/ages-stages-all -about-me.

CDC Certified Divorce Coaching® program. "Effective and Ineffective Actions." ©Divorce Coaching Inc. DCF-3, p 7.

Daramus, Aimee. "Video Games Can Be Used as a Therapy—Here's How." Psychreg. Last modified April 13, 2021. Accessed September 21, 2021. Psychreg.org/video-games-therapy.

Davis, Susan. "When Parenting Styles Differ." *Grow* by WebMD. Accessed August 2, 2021. WebMD.com/parenting/features/when-parenting-styles -differ.

Deater-Deckard, K., J. E. Lansford, K. A. Dodge, G. S. Pettit, and J. E. Bates. "The Development of Attitudes about Physical Punishment: An 8-Year Longitudinal Study." *Journal of Family Psychology* 17, no. 3 (2003): 351–60. doi.org/10.1037/0893-3200.17.3.351.

Docter, Pete, and Ronnie Del Carmen, dir. *Inside Out.* Burbank, CA: Walt Disney Studios Motion Pictures, 2015.

Ellis, Albert, and Debbie Joffe Ellis. *Rational Emotive Behavior Therapy.* American Psychological Association, 2011.

Fallis, Jordan. "How to Stimulate Your Vagus Nerve for Better Mental Health." January 21, 2017. Accessed September 20, 2021. SASS.UOttawa.ca/sites/sass.uottawa.ca/files/how_to_stimulate_your_vagus_nerve_for_better_mental_health_1.pdf.

Feeney, Judy. "The Systemic Nature of Couple Relationships: An Attachment Perspective." In *Attachment and Family Systems: Conceptual, Empirical, and Therapeutic Relatedness*, edited by Phyllis Erdman and Tom Caffery, 139–63. Routledge, 2015.

Goyal, Madhav, Sonal Singh, Erica M. S. Sibinga, Neda F. Gould, Anastasia Rowland-Seymour, Ritu Sharma, Zackary Berger, et al. "Meditation Programs for Psychological Stress and Well-Being: A Systematic Review and Meta-Analysis." *JAMA Internal Medicine* 174, no. 3 (January 6, 2014): 357–68. doi:10.1001/jamainternmed.2013.13018.

Karen, Robert. *Becoming Attached: First Relationships and How They Shape Our Capacity to Love*. New York: Oxford University Press, 1994.

Kessler, David. "The Five Stages of Grief." Grief.com. Accessed July 28, 2021. Grief.com/the-five-stages-of-grief.

Lisitsa, Ellie. "The Four Horsemen: Criticism, Contempt, Defensiveness, and Stonewalling." The Gottman Insitute. April 23, 2013. Accessed July 12, 2021. Gottman.com/blog/the-four-horsemen-recognizing-criticism-contempt-defensiveness-and-stonewalling.

McHale, James P., Allison Lauretti, Jean Talbot, and Christina Pouquette. "Retrospect and Prospect in the Psychological Study of Coparenting and Family Group Process." In *Retrospect and Prospect in the Psychological Study of Families*, edited by J. P. McHale and W. S. Grolnick, 127–65. Lawrence Erlbaum Associates Publishers, 2002.

Meyers, Seth. "How to Understand and Handle Bitter People." Psychology Today. October 7, 2019. Accessed September 21, 2021. PsychologyToday.com/us/blog/insight-is-2020/201910/how-understand-and-handle-bitter-people.

Minuchin, Salvador. *Families and Family Therapy*. Cambridge, MA: Harvard University Press, 1974.

Monroe, Jamison. "The Adolescent Brain on Meditation." Psychology Today. August 19, 2015. PsychologyToday.com/us/blog/the-guest-room/201508/the-adolescent-brain-meditation.

Morin, Amy. "15 Coping Strategies for Kids." Accessed September 21, 2021. VerywellFamily.com/coping-skills-for-kids-4586871.

Munoz, Alicia. "How to Co-Parent with an Ex Who Parents Differently." GoodTherapy.org. February 24, 2017. Accessed August 2, 2021. GoodTherapy.org/blog/how-to-co-parent-with-ex-who-parents-differently-0224175.

National Domestic Violence Hotline. "Create a Safety Plan." Accessed September 21, 2021. TheHotline.org/plan-for-safety/create-a-safety-plan.

OurFamilyWizard. "Five Reasons to Work with a Parenting Coordinator." Accessed September 21, 2021. OurFamilyWizard.com/blog/five-reasons-work-parenting-coordinator.

Parenting Agreement Checklist. Adapted from Protocol Resources for a Full Team Model: Collaborative Divorce, DC Metro Protocols Committee. September 2015.

Siegel, Daniel J., and Tina Payne Bryson. *The Whole-Brain Child: 12 Revolutionary Strategies to Nurture Your Child's Developing Mind.* New York: Delacorte Press, 2011.

Smith, Brendan L. "The Case against Spanking." American Psychological Association. April 2012. Accessed July 28, 2021. APA.org/monitor/2012 /04/spanking.

Smith, Sherry. "Co-Parenting Tips for a High Conflict Divorce. Featuring Dr. Tara Egan." *Stories of Divorce Resiliency*. Podcast audio. May 3, 2021. DivorceResiliency.com/season-1-episode-8.

Smith, Sherry. "Why Early Intervention is Crucial in Coparenting Your Kids. Featuring Lucy Dunning." *Stories of Divorce Resiliency*. Podcast audio. August 23, 2021. DivorceResiliency.com/stories-divorce-resiliency-season -2-episode-7.

Therapist Aid. "Parenting: Using Rewards and Punishments." Accessed August 2, 2021. TherapistAid.com/therapy-guide/parenting-rewards-punishments.

United Nations Human Rights Office of the High Commissioner. "Convention on the Rights of the Child." Accessed July 16, 2021. OHCHR.org/en /professionalinterest/pages/crc.aspx.

U.S. Department of Education. "Being an Effective Parent—Helping Your Child Through Early Adolescence." Last modified September 11, 2003. Accessed August 2, 2021. www2.Ed.gov/parents/academic/help/adolescence /part5.html.

Index

R

Relief, 115
Resentment, 114
Rewards and consequences system, 30–31
Role models, 5
Routines, 23

S

Sadness, 91–92, 113
Schedules, 33–34
Secure attachment, 10–11
Self-care, 127
Self-soothing techniques, 28, 76
Special events, 32–33
Structural Family Therapy, 7
Support groups, 126
Support networks, 122–124

T

Team-based approach to co-parenting, 7–8, 12
Technology detox, 94
Teens, mindfulness for, 94
Toxic exes, 61, 63
Triggers, 119

V

Vacations, 32–33
Values, 13
Vision boards, 128
Visualization, 116
Vulnerability, 21, 96, 110

Acknowledgments

I would like to acknowledge Dr. Tara Egan and Lucy Dunning for sharing their co-parenting expertise with me. These women work tirelessly and passionately to help others co-parent better for their kids. I would also like to thank my professors at Pfeiffer University, specifically Dr. George Bitar, Dr. Pearl Wong, and Dr. Deborah Lung, for teaching me how to heal my childhood trauma and change how I do relationships so I was able step into my calling and pay it forward.

About the Author

 **Sherry L. Smith,** LMFT, CDC®, is a psychotherapist, CDC Certified Divorce Coach®, co-parent coach, author, speaker, and podcast host. Combining her expertise in family systems, her training as a divorce coach, and her own life experience, Sherry has made the commitment to help people handle their breakup or divorce in a way that minimizes trauma for their kids. She believes early intervention creates a better outcome for the whole family.

In her spare time, she can be found meditating, hiking a mountain, trying out a new restaurant, listening to live music, or spending time with friends and family.

To learn more about Sherry, visit DivorceResiliency.com or check out her podcast, *Stories of Divorce Resiliency*, available anywhere you get your podcasts. She can also be found on Facebook or Instagram @divorceresiliency.